Dyatlov Nine:
Death Below Zero

catt dahman

J Ellington Ashton Press @ www.jellingtonashton.com
cattd.com

Dyatlov Nine:

Death Below Zero

The mysteries surrounding the deaths of nine young, experienced ski hikers in 1959 have never been solved. On a trip through the Ural Mountains, the group of students first were reported missing and then were found deceased, but several were not located until months following the tragedy. Despite exhaustive investigations, there has never been a theory that explains exactly what killed the nine, and because of this, many unusual conjectures have arisen.

Some accounts and beliefs are those based on the evidence, testimony, and logic. Others are imaginative and quite possible, but the authors of those have been almost discredited for having interpreted some evidence incorrectly, which doesn't necessarily mean that the central idea is incorrect. Other theories have covered very strange themes to include a yeti attack, UFOs, and teleportation. There are many who refuse to entertain any solution other than military/government causation and believe secret weapons testing, rogue missiles, or parachute mines are to blame. In the final group are those who think that radio waves or black holes are to blame.

Because of the truly strange behavior of the nine skiers, their shocking causes of death from autopsy reports and other evidence, and the many unanswered questions, the mystery has sparked fierce debates.

The fact is that we may never know exactly what happened to the young people during their trip and especially on February 1-2 of 1959.

I've had a maddening interest in Mount Everest and have done research for years as well as followed the yearly summits. Although the only common denominators would seem to be a mountain, snow and below freezing temperatures, and a group of physically fit, experienced, goal-driven people, facts and stories about Everest do cover the physical trauma of those recovered, and it was there that a theory was born.

It's been my habit to make theories fit evidence but never to make evidence fit theories. It keeps me honest. After gathering evidence (and there is a lot out there that is supposedly real but is really from a movie or documentary or that is improperly read from autopsy reports, or is from folklore), I laid it out and looked at a dozen possible theories. By working with an expert mountaineer, Brad Hammock, I eliminated several theories at once as he poked enormous holes in them. However, he also suggested some new ideas.

From there, my next expert jumped in; he has twenty years military experience and was able to add to the possible while dispelling others. Then, my expert on Russian history gave input, and DA Roberts, a Sheriff's deputy, helped me look at the crime scene, if there was one.

Add the fact that I came across some specific, not-oft quoted nor seen material, and the points lined up like magic. As the theory developed, my experts and I poked holes when we could, adjusted the theory to fit only the facts, and still had something that explained every single part of the unusual case.

It should be said that human error is normal for sensation seekers. As a scuba diver, I have taken foolish risks even though I am experienced and well-trained. Climbers on Everest take risks that in hindsight seemed illogical and have resulted in death. Why? Brad Hammock explains that when people are both sensation seekers, looking for that high of conquering and testing themselves and the goal is threatened, they take risks. In no way should human error, in my account, be taken as meaning that the Dyatlov Nine *deserved* their fate, were poor at their sport, or were to blame; in ordinary circumstances, human error might never have caused their deaths.

Nature played a critical role in the deaths, yet we can't say that in normal circumstances it would have been anything but an inconvenience.

There is a reason that no single theory has fit all the evidence; it was not one single event that caused the heart-breaking deaths. An imperfect storm arose and snowballed; if we use a cliché, a series of events lined up in a chain of events, a storm of events that was formed by both humans and nature.

Imperfect because not one of the elements would have killed the nine: the storm shows itself partly in several theories, and that is because no single event was to blame. If I am correct, then at dozens of points, had there been an intervention in the chain of events, all or some of the group would have survived to tell about what *almost happened*.

Unfortunately, there was no intervening event, and the storm of events took its toll. In all its imperfection was a storm of ferocious force and death occurred below zero.

Part I

1

The Characters

Originally, there were ten on the trip, but one of the hikers/skiers/mountaineers (called tourists at that time) was forced to turn back due to medical issues.

The Mountain expedition was planned so that everyone of the tourists could gain his level 3 certification for hiking/skiing. That was the highest level available, and summiting Mount Otorten in the conditions in January-February of that year would allow all of them to become experts. It was a demanding goal since sudden snow storms, isolation, below freezing temperatures, primitive supplies by modern standards, strong winds, and magnetic anomalies that made compass use difficult were the usual.

While the mountain wasn't difficult by technicality (it could be climbed or skied but didn't require crampons and alpine climbing) nor critically difficult as far as altitude, both wind funnels and the cold, unpredictable weather made it a very difficult summit.

Natives avoided the upper reaches because there were no trees or life, a lack of game to hunt, and high, unexpected winds and polar temperatures.

The Ural Polytechnical Institute where the tourists were associated authorized the expedition and paid for almost all supplies and travel. The objectives, besides the certification, were to learn about the nature and economy of the northern lands, to educate and interest the public at home and abroad, to improve hiking and skiing skills, and to test the depth of soil freezing in the Northern Urals.

The university had faith in the tourists:

"All members were eligible for a hike with this difficulty. Each of them had experience in winter hiking of II-nd category of difficulty, and the leader of the group Dyatlov had experience in the winter expeditions of III-rd category of difficulty to the Polar Ural. Dyatlov had the experience of three nights in a treeless area in Mt Manaragi area. We can judge the experience of the group members by the reference given by UPI sport club".

Igor Dyatlov was the leader of the expedition with three former level 3 hikes, three level 2s, and three level 1s and was highly respected by the others for his leadership ability; some called him the best hiker at the university. A radio engineering student at Ural Polytechnical Institute, he was focused on his studies. Not only was he an expert at building lighter, more portable radios which were still too heavy and large to be carried on an expedition in 1959, he also engineered the heater that was used to warm the tent, and he designed the tent itself, forming a large tent from two smaller tents.

He often looked out of place in photographs when posed for the camera, as if he didn't belong in that moment or in that environment. On a mountain, his entire persona changed. No longer was he under rules of the government and society; he was free and *in charge*. His word was law when he led because lives depended on his decisions.

The outdoors was his true element, and he was able to make excellent decisions based on what he saw in his surroundings.

Sometimes he took risks, sometimes he made difficult choices, but he was reliable and goal-driven when hiking and skiing. At twenty-three, he was intelligent and mature but not without a good sense of humor and a love of fun. He had an ability to easily get along with others. People liked Igor.

Igor & Yuri
w/ Zina

going
with
Zina
Possible
&
Love affair

Although some have said he "wasn't the most handsome" of the group, he had an interesting face, an honest face that inspired trust. The whites of his eyes near his nose show very well; some experts indicate this is a sign of a calmness.

He was not bulky muscular but had wiry muscles born of physical activity such as skiing   and hiking.

Note the calm eye expression and wide smile.
He looks excited and confident. His backpack
is stuffed full, and the weight is worn in the top
of the pack (with men) because of the center of
gravity. Women wear weight lower in packs.
He is warmly dressed.

Zanaida Kolmogorova (Zina) was also a student of radio engineering. She was twenty-two, beautiful, loved by all, respected, and was the heart of the expedition. She previously had dated Yuri Doroshenko who was also on the expedition but currently, in some way, she was involved with Igor Dyatlov (he carried a picture of her in his journal). Her heart was torn. It is possible that Igor was more emotionally involved than she. She hid her feelings as well as she could.

During the trip, she enjoyed prompting debates about love, commented (in her diary) about several of the men, and romantically idealized some of the party. It's likely that she was more in love with the idea of love than in love.

Possible Instigator ?

Zina had garnered a lot of respect on a previous hike that left her bitten by a viper and very ill. Instead of giving up, she not only fought the poison, but also insisted on carrying her own part of the group's load and apologized often for slowing the other hikers and causing them to worry. It is said that she never cried despite the tremendous pain. Her experience included one each level 1s and 3s and four level 2s.

She never met a stranger, and everyone seemingly was drawn to her: men, women, and especially children. She was an entertainer, loved to sing, and always wanted everyone to be happy. People were so drawn to her that they swore they already knew her.

* Had Relationship
w/ 2-Prior
members of the
Team.
△-Love affair
Problems?

Lyudmila Dubinina (Lyuda) was a very pretty blonde student at UPI with a major in economics.

If Dyatlov were the leader and Zina the heart, Lyuda was the compass for everything considered right in that era. She was driven in her studies, athletic, but feminine, and healthy, pure, and a staunch, outspoken Communist; she frequently made it clear that she supported the Communist party in all ways. She was never afraid to share her loyalty.

She was also strong in personality, and had the expedition been forced to depend on a second leader, she was strong-willed enough to lead, although at time, she did worry that some thought her too young. It was Lyuda who was treasurer for the expedition, and she was the one who organized everything. It's clear that she was considered very responsible.

Her experiences included a level 1 and three level 2s.

Yuri Doroshenko (Yuri) was twenty-one and had once dated Zina, but he had broken up with her. Why he ended the relationship was a mystery, but he seemed fine with Zina and Igor having a close friendship that might be developing into something more.

Both the tallest and poorest of the group, he was also the bravest. He had proven this when Zina once screamed a warning and he chased a bear away from camp with only a geologist's hammer. This bravery shown to "save" Zina from the creature, serious talks, and general fun led to them date and meet one another's families.

He was also a radio engineering student and avid hiker-skier but sometimes couldn't afford the clothing necessay to keep him warmly dressed. He told others that his mother had been saving money for over a year to buy him a proper, warm coat.

In some photos such as those above, he looks very serious. Note that while some might wonder why Zina chose a very poor man when she had her pick of boyfriends, examination of his photos reveal that his features are often cited as desirable by women: his cleft chin, full, well-shaped lips, and expressive eyes.

Yuri's exact level of experience is unknown, but he had hiked and skied. (Zina called him Yurda instead of Yuri, meaning that their relationship was very close. Nicknames change according to relationships.)

Above, kneeling on the left, he looks very physically
fit, alert, happy, and handsome.

Yuri Krivonischenko (Georgy) was a graduate of the university with a degree in civil engineering and hydraulics and was almost twenty-four when he died. Also, he had previously worked as an engineer at a nuclear plant and did clean-up after the nuclear contamination at Kyshtym.

degree
Civil
Engin
worked in
Nuclear
Plant -
Govt. Connect ?

c

A jokester and entertainer, he played a mandolin on the trip and enjoyed singing. He liked to show-off when the students met at his parents' large apartment where they were always welcomed to play music, talk about school and friends, or debate various topics. His parents were well-educated and involved in the community and enjoyed seeing the young people gather for entertainment and deep discussions about the world.

His face was babyish for his age but very expressive. By all accounts, he was cheerful and fun. A friend of Dyatlov, he knew all the hikers well except for one. Before they reached the mountain, he started joking around, pretending to be a panhandler as he played the mandolin and sang. The police almost arrested him, kept him in jail, and saved his life, but his antics didn't save his life.

He was brave, self-motivated, unselfish, and tenacious about earning certifications outdoors; everything in nature fascinated him, especially those which challenged his abilities.

Georgy's mountaineering experience is unclear.
(Georgios is the Greek form of Yuri and became a nickname)

Alexander Kolevatov (Sasha) had majored in metallurgy, moved to Moscow, and worked in a building called only I 3394. After that, he was a part of working toward the nuclear agenda. Only working did he join the UPI as a physics major. At both universities he was a member of the hiking clubs and had extensive experience in the polar region.

His handsome features and classic looks speak to the fact that he was one of the wealthiest of the group, worldly, and very serious., but It wasn't always that good for him. His father died in a mysterious way, in a railway, killed by a train. The family lost everything and was barely kept alive by his sister's work as a teacher. He was what we now call "home-schooled".

After attending the university, in Moscow and then attending UPI, he had money, dressed well, and smoked a pipe with real tobacco. He had completed three level 1 hikes, one level 2, and one level 3.

He was twenty-four when he died, methodical and responsible, mature and intelligent. Because of his relative wealth, life experience, or sophistication, the others looked upon what he said and did with some awe, and to them, he seemed far older and more mature.

(Sasha is a common nickname for those named Alexander because of the SA sound and diminutive -sha added)

Due to his age, Education, WORK history and financial funds He may well have been working undercover as a NKVD (or KGB) agent.

Rustem Slobodin (Rustik) was twenty-three, played the mandolin, loved hiking, and was a graduate of UPI. Although he was Russian, he was given an Asian name because he was born there while his parents, both professors, were working abroad.

He was the most physically fit. He led many sports teams at the university and loved long-distance running, always pushing himself to run faster and farther. An avid hiker and skier, he enjoyed hiking with his father to very inhospitable areas and testing himself in harsh environments, around hostile natives, and forcing his body and mind to adapt to extremes.

He was likely the most adventurous of the expedition and a risk-taker; he was very self-confident and had accomplished one level 3 expedition, three 2s and two 1s

He does NOT strike me as anything more than adventurous and egotistical young man. Looks are deceiving but we will never know.

Due to family history
he may have been watched.

Seems to be somewhat
of an artistic person.

Nicolai Thibeaux-Brignolles (Kolya), twenty-three, began and ended life in heartbreaking ways. Although the family was an aristocratic one from France and was Communist, Kolya's father did something to offend Stalin and was sent away to a prison camp for revolutionists, a prison for hard labor. His sentence was for ten years, and he died there. The family was left without a provider and with a stigma. But Kolya didn't let that hold him back.

A

A graduate of UPI with a major in civil engineering, he also was an experienced hiker and skier with three level 1s, two level 2s, and a single level 3. He was considered to be friendly, most helpful, and humorous.

(Kolya is a nickname for Nicolai or in English, Nicholas. It's clearer when the end of the name is isolated: Cola or Colya to Kolya)

Semyon Zolotaryov was one of the most interesting of the group. He was thirty-seven or thirty-eight years old and had tried to get an engineering degree, but each time he enrolled, the program downsized. The degree he obtained later was in physical education.

OK;
Here we have
a 38 yr. old
who failed to get
his engineering
degree yet;
Served on front
Lines of WWII
and won
several awards
despite fact
he was COSSAK.

He was a
club-105 when
a student fell
ill.
who was he
working for?

He served in the war on the front lines at a time when the survival rate was about 3 percent; he won four awards (not generally given to Cossacks), and was an experienced guide for mountaineering, hiking, and skiing.

Besides his age, other traits set him apart from the others of the group. He was tattooed and single (unusual for his age). He was a last-minute addition to the group when a student wasn't allowed to go because of schoolwork, and none of the group members knew Semyon before the ill-fated trip. He was eventually accepted by most of the tourists and seemed to enjoy himself.

Yuri Yudin was also on the expedition, but at the last village before they left civilization, he was suffering severe pain from chronic sciatica. At twenty-two, he was well liked by everyone and was an experienced hiker and skier. He was especially liked by the two women of the group. He had experienced one level 3, two level 2s, and three level 1s.

Yuri offered a few theories but was traumatized by having to identify personal possessions and may have suffered survivor's guilt. He lived to be seventy-five and always questioned what had happened to cause the tragedy.

2

1.23.59

January 23, 1959

Ten tourists took the train from Sverdlovsk to Serov. Regardless of how prepared they were, their nerves and excitement caused them to wonder where items were packed, if at all. Each member of the group had to carry a certain amount of weight, so every item had to be necessary or it wasn't packed.

Lyuda wondered if she, the accountant and organizer, had spent foolishly for supplies, and when she feared they had forgotten something vital, she rechecked every pack. She was so concerned and checked everything so often that they almost didn't have time to tell everyone goodbye and get to the train station. They arrived with little time to spare and had to, again, tell more people goodbye. She wrote *"Just before our departure, those who wanted to say goodbye came to meet us. We were really short of time but arrived at the railway station with seconds to spare. Then we had to say goodbye to everyone."*

Of everything, food was the one supply they had plenty of. Lyuda planned for them to buy only a few extras, such as fresh bread, along the way. The university had failed to provide enough chocolate for their energy needs, but coffee with sugar would suffice.

"It begins," Igor said, grinning, so happy that the trip had begun that he forgot to keep his lips closed over the slight gap in his upper front teeth that sometimes made him self-conscious. "We'll be on the summit before long."

"And all together, we'll get our certification. Good friends, indeed." Sasha said, unable to light his pipe on the train, so he chewed the stem. He enjoyed showing a stern demeanor, but he was unable to hide a big, broad grin; he cheered as he saw their train.

Once on the Number 43 train, Zina displayed her wickedly good sense of humor as she asked Sasha, "Do you need a cigarette then?" Later, when she wrote in her diary, she wondered: *The boys solemnly swore not to smoke the entire trip. I wonder how much will-power they have to get by without cigarettes?* At least two of the men would not resist the temptation of tobacco while on the trip.

Another group of hikers rode with the ten, and most were already friends with the Dyatlov's group. It was thrilling to be in a large, like-minded group. They discussed their travel plans, their hiking routes, classmates, and life. They talked about love and friendship. Along with another group of tourists, the ten in Dyatlov's group sang as the men played mandolins.

Semyon Zolotaryov was still getting to know those with him but thought he understood the basic personalities.

He thought Igor Dyatolov was a natural leader who never wavered in his decisions, but also never made anyone feel foolish for making suggestions. He was reserved around Semyon but still warm; in time, they could become good friends, he hoped.

Zina Kolmogorova seemed to be very close to Igor, but if there were a romance, it was secret, and he seemed more invested than did she. She was a great person, friendly and positive, no matter the situation. Zina was also brilliant and beautiful with the most expressive eyes Semyon had ever seen.

Yuri Doroshenko clearly cared more about Zina than he would a friend. Semyon thought he was brave and protective, the type who would never back down when he defended a belief or a friend. Obviously, he was not well-off; in fact, he seemed poor, but he was treated no differently and didn't seem awed by those who were better off. Fearless. He tended to watch Zina a lot.

Semyon had to remind himself that Krivonischenko liked to be called Georgy to distinguish him from the other two Yuris. He was humorous and mischievous, and one of the most welcoming people in the group. He was also loyal and protective and a naturally funny person; he didn't even have to try to make people laugh.

Sasha Kolevatov was reserved and the least welcoming. He was intense, always deep in thought, and a kind of "father figure" to everyone in the group. He wasn't quite snobbish because he was far too nice, but he was cooler in attitude toward Semyon.

Rustik was by far the most muscular and physically fit and confident to the point of near-arrogance, yet he smiled a lot and treated the others like family. Of everyone, he was the only one who would dare to question Igor Dyatlov although he hadn't yet. He watched everyone and everything; nothing got by his notice.

Kolya Thibeaux-Brignolles was the most open, honest, and simple. He said what he felt and spoke up, but he was tasteful and respectful when he did so. The women treated him as a pet, and for some reason, no matter what the case, no one ever became irritated with him. Semyon didn't know the man well enough to guess why this was, but Kolya was beloved. He was also very humorous. It was possible his good looks endeared him to the ladies.

Georgy was also a bit of a pet, as humorous as a Kolya, and always cheerful; he was also a hard worker, often offering to help others with chores. His tenacity for reaching goals had to be something he was both born with and had learned because Georgy never saw defeat. He only saw possibilities and achievements.

And Lyuda. She was very mature and could be quiet, but then she also had a sly, humorous side. She was an over-achiever. Semyon didn't know what to think of her, but he was reserved when around her because he was sure she disliked him for some reason. Maybe she didn't care for a stranger joining them or perhaps he had offended her in some way, but her attitude toward him was mostly cold. Only a few times had she smiled and shown warmth, so she may not have wanted to like him, but at times, accepted him reluctantly. She wavered in her treatment of him.

There was a lot to consider regarding the group's dynamics.

Semyon was an unknown factor to them, and Lyuda and the rest had already discussed the point that none wanted him to come with them since he was a stranger. He didn't know them and their ways. They were so accustomed to one another they read each other's moods easily, knew strengths and weaknesses, were proven, and were at ease with one another. He was a stranger to them; they were strangers to him. Why had he wanted to join them except to get his level 3 certification? = *They Suspected him as expert*

He was correct that some were unwilling to be friends yet.

Lyuda knew that there wasn't really a choice since it wasn't for them to decide who went on the expedition that was paid for by the university. She wrote in her journal: *but then we all agreed, because you can't refuse.*

Semyon tried his best to fit in as they made up new songs. "Let me help you. I'll try to keep up by writing them down." He won smiles, even from Lyuda.

They fell asleep as the sound of the train lulled them. The taiga, or coniferous forest near the tundra, was dark.

The land was both claustrophobic and agoraphobic because the trees seemed to swallow everything and they grew thickly in lower areas, but the white landscape went on forever and touched the snow-filled sky. The ice, ten feet deep in places, hid secrets. Zina wrote: *"Everybody is falling asleep, and behind the window, Ural taiga is spread in all direction."*

Supplies that each carried were as follows:

- Each member: backpack, boots and extra laces, felt (tent) boots, gaiters or boot wraps, several pairs of cotton and wool socks, a belted, quilted jacket, two sweaters, a hat, balaclava (face covering or mask), knife, spoon, bowl, cup, toiletries, journal and pencil, matches, extra pants, underwear, a scarf, skies and poles, insoles, blanket.
- Some carried binoculars, a compass, pictures, cameras, and other personal items. Georgy and Kolya carried Finnish knives that were considered illegal weapons. Sasha's Finnish knife was legal, sanctioned by the police. Semyon carried a Finnish knife, too, legal or illegal not known.
- Group load that was divided among the tourists: large tent, cooking utensils, food, two-handled saw, several axes, buckets, a first aid kit, spare skies, a repair kit of tools, matches, candles, flashlights, a heater and the pipe vents (designed by Igor), maps, a group journal, rope, and a thermometer.

I still Believe Semyon was a KGB Plant.

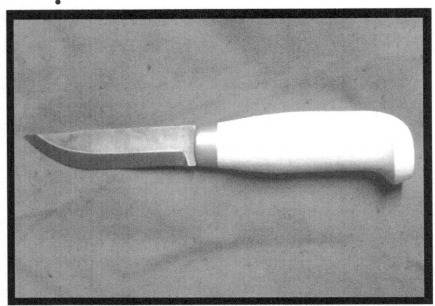

Finnish Knife

3

1.24.59

January 24, 1959

It was seven in the morning when they arrived in Servo.

"Watch this," Georgy Krivonishenko said. Taking the mandolin in hand, he began singing at the station, pretending to panhandle for money. Some people were amused when he held out his cap, but others frowned.

The town was known for well-behaved Communist citizens who did not panhandle, didn't break the law, and were not loud in public places. Georgy had to plead ignorance and beg forgiveness when the police arrived and took him to the station. Zina wrote: *"Yuri Kriv was taken to the police station. He wanted to raise money for candy. It was funny."* He could have been charged with disturbing the peace and put in jail, but he was let go with a stern warning. To prevent another arrest for loitering or something worse, the tourists left the station since their next train wasn't until 6:30 PM, and they were not allowed to remain at the train station.

Of the incident, Yuri Yudin wrote, *"At the station we were met with hell of a hospitality. They didn't allow us into the building. The policeman stares at us suspiciously. There is no crime or vandalism in the city, as it supposed to be in times of Communism. And then Yuri Krivo started a song; the cops grabbed him and took him away."*

Because they couldn't go far with all the equipment, it's pure luck that at a local school, they were allowed to go inside and cook a meal for themselves. The custodian allowed them to use a storage room for their belongings and brought them water to make tea. To return the favor, the group spoke to school children in grades one and two about their travels, teaching them about equipment, answering questions, and singing.

"Who has been camping before?" Zina asked. Children raised their hands and called out. She had to explain the kind of camping that they planned, carrying everything with them in large backpacks, travelling for hours on skies, and sleeping in a tent in the freezing temperatures.

By the time the tourists were ready to leave, the children were so taken with the group, especially Zina, that they made a fuss until allowed to go with their new friends to the station. Some children burst into tears.

Yudin wrote in the group's diary:

"In the interval between 1st and 2nd shifts in school we organized meeting with pupils. The room crammed with so many curious children. Zolotaryov: "Kids, I will tell you now... Tourism is, enables you to..." Everyone is still, quiet, engaged. Z. Kolmogorova: Tra- ta- ta- ta, what's your name, you went where, awesome, you have been camping, she went on and on...Questions didn't end. We had to explain and show to every kid everything, from torches to tents. It took us 2 hours, and kids didn't want to let us go. They sang songs to each other. The whole school saw us at the station. Everything ended as expected; when we were leaving, the kids yelled and cried, asking Zina to stay with them. They promised to behave and study well."

"Don't leave us," a little boy begged Zina. "Stay here. Please stay and sing with us."

"I'll see you again, but you must behave and study hard. Promise," Zina said. She hugged them.

"They love you," Igor commented. "Everyone does."

There was no more time to think about the children; they had to get on the train. Lyuda, small, crawled under the seat to save the fare. Everyone laughed. When it was safe to crawl out, she joined her friends, and they made a meal of garlic bread and water.

After that, they entertained themselves by singing a while and talking.

"Give it back," a man approached and demanded. He was drunk, angry, and spoiling for a fight and suddenly had walked over to the group from another area.

"What is that? Give what back to you?" Rustik asked the other man who was tottering a little on his feet. If the man demanded a fight or bothered the women, he was prepared to fight. He glanced at Yuri and Igor who gave him quick nods; they would handle the man's friends if the need arose.

"My bottle." The stranger glared. "Someone took it from my pocket."

Only after Rustik asked questions did he and the rest understand the problem. The drunken man thought that Dyatlov's group stole a bottle of vodka from him, and if he didn't get it back, he would punch someone in his teeth.

Rustik shrugged. They were without liquor other than the small medicinal flask they carried and had sworn off cigarettes; a bottle of vodka would have been welcomed, but they didn't have it. No one stole it. Rustik explained that they had not stolen the bottle and explained that they weren't drinking, so the man went away when Rustik threatened to call the police.

"Good thing he left since we don't need two visits from the police," Georgy said. He blushed, recalling his own brush with the law.

"Let's forget the whole thing. Let's talk about love."

The men groaned.

Zina continued, "Let's discuss what love is."

"I'm not sure I've ever been in love," Lyuda admitted.

Kolya grinned. "That's why we must discuss it, I suppose. Love is complicated."

When Zina suggested that they also talk about kisses, the men began to speak out, expressing their opinions. Everyone hooted until tears began.

Semyon felt a kinship as he and many others laughed so hard that tears streamed down their faces. Seeing the discomfort and embarrassment of some of the men was very comical.

Lyuda laughed at them as they began to speak over one another. "What do you think, Sasha?"

Sasha Kolevatov thought as he smoked his pipe and considered the matters of the heart. Everyone watched his face, waiting. When he started to speak, he went on for a long time, explaining his beliefs, adding how he thought kisses should be. "Instead of kissing to find the right one, a man should kiss the woman, and vice versa, that he *knows* is the one."

Lyuda declared him the winner of the debate and later wrote: *Probably he expressed not only his own thoughts, but anyway, he obviously won.*

Yuri quickly glanced at Zina; then, he nodded. "I'd only kiss the one I loved."

- Author's note: The facts are not entirely clear if the group carried any liquor. It would not have been mentioned in the journals because the group journal had to be turned in to the university. Testimonies indicate that Zina and Yuri told of having fun without alcohol when at parties and dances. There is a discrepancy whether the search and rescue team found alcohol and consumed it or if there were none found.

4

1.25.59

January 25, 1959

At Vizhay, the Dyatlov ten parted ways with the other tourist group.

All but Yuri Doroshenko and Sasha Kolevatov went to the cinema to see a musical, and the other eight returned to the hostel, singling at the tops of their lungs and the talk, again, turned to love but also dancing and friendship. Igor, surprisingly, did a little dance that made everyone laugh. He was a great skier and hiker but not a good dancer. The musical was one of their favorites, and they knew all the words to the songs.

"Stop singing, Igor," Lyuda begged, smiling. She later noted: *"We are extremely lucky! The Symphonie in Gold was showing. We left all our things and packs at the hotel and went to the club. The image was a bit fuzzy, but it didn't overshadow the pleasure at all. Yurka Krivo, sitting next to me, was smacking his lips and oohing with delight. This is real happiness, so difficult to describe with words. The music is just fabulous! The mood after the movie greatly improved. Igor Dyatlov was unrecognizable. He tried to dance and even started singing."*

Sasha wrote: *"After dinner, which was held in a warm "friendly atmosphere," we moved to the "hotel", which was the usual hut with three windows. We went to the cinema, leaving "home" Doroshenko and Kolevatov. We watched as The Symphonie in Gold came back in "musical mood". Now we are busy getting ready the equipment."*

Lyuda was unsure why Zina and Yuri broke up but felt that Yuri was not a bad person. She wrote: *Yurka is still a good-natured person, at least, judging by his behavior.* As a woman, she recognized that Zina had feelings for her former boyfriend as well as for Igor; sometimes people wanted what they couldn't have more than what they could. At least the three didn't let emotions get in the way of the trip.

When talk turned to freedom, *svoboda*, Lyuda became uncomfortable; to her, it was a useless discussion because in the end, the idea didn't matter. What *was* freedom, anyway? Were they not free to enjoy the trip and make choices? Too much freedom led to poor choices which were harmful to society, the government, and themselves. It wasn't a topic she wanted to consider.

She was quiet as she ate her noodles and wondered why they had to have such deep discussions.

The tourists eating in a café in Vezhay, their last civilized meal.

5

1.5.59

January 26, 1959

The temperature was -17 C or 1 F. Cold. Sasha made a note of the experience: *"We did not boil water in the morning, wood was damp. In the evening it took us 6 hours to boil the water. Had breakfast in the dining room, goulash and tea. When they handed us the lukewarm tea, Dyatlov said with a smile: 'If the tea is cold, then go out and drink it on the street; it will be hot.' Original thought."*

Left to right, back: Yuri Doroshenko, Yuri Yudin, Igor, Kolya , front: Zina (with most of her face covered), Lyuda, Semyon, and Rustik. Georgy took the picture and Sasha is not in view. Semyon and Rustik seem to be handling the cold the best.

They traveled to Settlement 41 by GAZ-63, a truck, by riding in the back where they almost froze. It was a miserable three hours of travel, but it saved a great deal of time.

At Settlement 41, the group stayed in the pine-log barrackers where woodcutters lived.

To their shock, the men who lived in the barracks were very intelligent. One, Ognev, nicknamed The Beard because of his lush, red beard, was the most intelligent, best read, most well-spoken, and wise, and he was a true romantic. He was twenty-seven but acted far older. Zina wrote: *"We arrived at the 41st settlement. Workers are simply working here, not prisoners, but recruits. There are many smart ones."*

Lyuda was so intimidated that she listened to the men talk about work and life and recite poetry but was reluctant to mention her own views. She feared she might say something foolish; it was a terrible anxiety for anyone thinking that she was immature or silly.

The Beard is cute, she thought, and she was very quiet around him. *"Rustik and Kolya reasoned a little about everything, about work, etc. I like these guys. A big difference between them, graduated from the institute Rustik, Ko, Yurda and us. All the same, their judgments are more mature and smarter than ours. My God, I do not even talk about mine."*

"Do you feel all right, Lyuda?" Semyon asked, hoping to cause her to like him a little more. She was still quiet around him, and he wanted her friendship; she had a beautiful personality.

"I'm fine. Thank you. Are you going to watch the movies, play music and sing, or write in your journal?" Lyuda asked.

"I think I'll listen to Rustik and Kolya debate. One of them might need some help. Maybe you could help as well." Semyon appealed to her intelligence.

Lyuda blushed, despising the fact that she did. She was the youngest; no one wanted her views. She couldn't share. "No, thank you. I want to write in my diary." She did so and noted that her mood had turned down and would remain so for a while. For her, her inability to know everything she wished to know was pure hell.

Zina also enjoyed The Beard's discussion and Rustik's mandolin playing, as well as the singing, but was troubled by a specific event. Her former boyfriend, Yuri Doroshenko, gave her his mittens to wear, but she felt uncomfortable. Igor might be jealous, or it might seem she was taking advantage of a former flame.

"Why didn't you take the mittens?" Lyuda asked.

Zina shrugged. "Why did he offer them to me? He broke up with me. How can we just be friends now?"

Lyuda smiled. "Don't make it more than it is," he offered, "so accept them to borrow. Sometimes we can't have life as we want."

"I want a man fully or not at all," Zina said as she frowned. "I'm confused about why he's being so nice to me now."

"Just wear the mittens for your hands. Not for your heart," Lyuda suggested.

Zina thanked Yuri and wore the mittens.

Lyuda was a little smitten by The Beard and wrote: *Especially memorable among all is Ognev with a red beard and the nickname of his "Beard". In general, very rarely are there such people in such a hole. A true romantic, a geologist and generally well-rounded.*

And Zina wrote: *Many workers are very talented, intelligent people. Especially "the beard", his beard is ginger, ginger, and his eyes are also ginger, and brown.*

(The word for *beard*, in Russian, is *boroda*.)

Nicotine withdrawal was difficult for several of the group. Kolya wrote in the group diary and admitted that he was unable to abstain; he had sneaked a few cigarettes and wrote: *I can't, although I tried. Nick Thibeaux.*

Kolya fell in the snow when he played the comic

6

1.27.59

January 27, 1959

The weather was good with wind to the tourists' backs. They bought loaves of soft, warm bread from the workers, and some men copied illegal songs called *prison songs*. Smiling all the while, the workers and the tourists traded little gifts. Ognev carefully explained to Igor the direction to take once in the next camp and how to find the right cabin to sleep in.

The tourists were around the Mansi, people who are native to the region and are hunters and gatherers. Some taught the group native words that were written into journals. One very interesting aspect of the natives was that the shamans collected fly agaric which is a kind of mushroom that is intoxicating. While it can kill a person, who ingests it in its raw form, it can be dried and eaten in small quantities or filtered in an unusual way. Reindeer love fly agaric and eat it as often as they find it growing under pine trees. Sipping deer urine after a deer consumes the mushroom is safer. Most shamans settled for tiny amounts of the dried version.

The Dyatlov group was ready to go to the next location but had to wait for their next mode of transportation to eat hay. One of the workers at the camp brought around a well-fed horse with a sleigh to carry their backpacks. It was a chance to ski and stretch their skiing muscles without carrying heavy packs. Yuri D said of it: *"Horse is slow. What a pleasure to go without backpacks. We covered 8 km in 2 hours. It's getting dark. The horse is causing the delay."*

They called the driver Uncle Slava. Yuri Yudin wished there were enough room for him in   the sleigh alongside the backpacks because his back ached so badly. Something he had suffered from for years, the pain in his spine and down his legs was excruciating and growing worse. Sciatica. He told the others he knew he would hold them back and the only choice was for him to go back home and miss the trip. Everyone expressed dismay since he was well-liked by all, especially the women. He decided to go to the next stop with them but then return home.

He was heart-sick but kept a cheerful smile on his face and refused to make his friends feel bad.

They were thrilled to be skiing through such beautiful scenery. The horse drawn sleigh enabled them to travel almost five miles in two hours. Despite that, it was a fifteen-mile journey, and it was dark in the next settlement when they arrived.

Yuri Yudin is probably the figure seen far to the right and last. He is in pain and unable to keep up even without a pack.

The abandoned geological site was made up of dozens of houses and huts but only one was fit for overnight use. The miners and families had left the town long before, leaving it empty of life. Yuri Doroshenko wrote: *Only one is suitable for living. In complete darkness, we found a village and the house. We started a fire with wood boards. Smoke came from the stove. Several people hurt their hands on old nails. Everything is well. We were talking and joking till 3 in the morning.*

The cabin was harsh, very cold, and dirty, but it was better than nothing. The group downplayed the work required to spend the night in the cabin. While Zina and Lyuda organized the supplies, the men trudged over to the other delipidated cabins to gather boards, sometimes prying them loose with the axes. Their hands were dotted with nails that cut their hands and slashed cuts. The work was worth it; they were warm and were able to make a late dinner supplemented with the left-over two loaves of bread.

*Author's note. To treat their injuries, they had a good first aid kit. Some items included were as follows: bandages, gauze, scissors, alcohol, iodine, aspirin, vitamins, Vaseline, and a medicinal flask of vodka.

7

1.28.59

January 28, 1959

It was 8 C outside (46 F). Warm.

Yuri Yudin tried to push through his pain, but he knew he had made the right decision to go back home. He would only have slowed the group if he went along, and if his back got worse, he would be a burden that they would have to carry, cutting the trip short. In fact, the pain had worsened. After gathering pyrite and quartz for his geology interests and for the university, he prepared to return to the village and await his friends' return. The tourists took his load and divided it among their packs. One of those items was the first aid kit because Yudin had overseen everything medical.

Lyuda was particularly upset about Yudin's leaving and wrote: *It is a pity, of course, that he leaves us. Especially for me and Zina, but nothing can be done about it.*

Reluctant to rush Yuri Yudin to go back so they could begin the expedition, the others waited for him to find his rocks and minerals, causing another late start. Igor told Yuri Yudin that instead of February 12, the group planned to return February 14 because of the delays, and they wished him good health.

Following the river Lozya, the tourists were forced to stop and scrape *wet, melting snow* from their skis. The terrain was flat and heavily forested and breathtakingly beautiful.

It was between 4:00 and 5:30 when they stopped to eat, but afterward, they continued their travel in order to make up for a late start.

They saw signs of native people, the Mansi who were peaceful and welcoming to strangers.

Despite being in a positive frame of mind when they stopped to make camp, tiny cracks appeared within the group. Igor Dyatlov had realized something important. Although he cared deeply for Zina and had kissed her before, he knew that she was meant to be only a close friend to him. She and Yuri had a strong history and whatever caused them to break up had faded. He stayed close to her, and she often looked at him. They laughed together. Igor understood, but it made him tense, and he brushed her off and ignored her; it was the best for all three involved. He had to put distance between them.

Zina was unhappy with Igor Dyatlov and wrote: *Igor was rude the whole evening; I just couldn't recognize him. I had to sleep on the wood near the stove.*

The journals were both wonderful to have and a curse.

The nine skier/ hikers were unable to express their most basic thoughts as they looked at the Ural Mountains while they prepared to summit Mount Otorten, a 190-mile journey. The beauty of the slopes, the snow, the trees, and the sky was impossible to put into the right words. There was no possible way to explain an overload of senses and the feeling in the soul that came with the sights. It was in all ways, breathtaking.

What could they write about? Little, probably.

After successfully making their trip, each would be rated a level 3, a very impressive feat. But to get the change in status, the venture needed to go smoothly so that they could show their abilities. Mistakes in camping techniques, skiing, or navigation couldn't be written about, so it was better to adjust, repair, and skip the notes. They had to show expertise in first aid and survival if the worst happened and those were needed, but to need either of those skills might cause a problem in their certification. Catch-22.

An upbeat attitude was desired. It was good to write about how fun, positive, smart, and industrious the teammates were. It was acceptable to laughingly make teasing remarks about the others if nothing were personal, nasty, or cruel. Sometimes, that left nothing to write about since seven men and two women were likely to argue or to scrape the nerves of their friends.

It was 1959. In the Soviet Union. The group was made up of excellent communist youths, and individuals were unimportant; the whole mattered. The collective being was greater than the lone person. To suggest a friend was acting in a non-group-centric manner might doom that friend to serious trouble; to show oneself being overly critical showed a lack of comradeship.

That night, the men put together the heater that Igor designed and then sewed curtains for the tent. Igor waved Zina away. "Go sing by the fire. Rustik can teach you to play the mandolin."

Her feelings were hurt, but she forced a smile and asked Rustik to show her how to play a song.

Lyuda: "Today, we spend our first night in the tent. The guys are busy with the stove or sewing curtains out of sheets. With some thing(s) completed and others not, we sit for dinner. After dinner, we sit for long time around the campfire and sing heartfelt songs. Zina even tries to learn to play the mandolin under guidance of our musician, Rustik."

The heater Igor designed warmed the tent and was vented; Igor Dyatlov had designed the tent for a large group of twelve. Each night, someone slept close to the stove to make sure nothing went wrong. The first night, Yuri was on duty, but he grew angry because the stove was too hot. Cursing, he moved away from the heat and argued about having to sleep so close to the stove. He was unhappy with having to sleep in a hot place, and he expressed himself dramatically.

"You're all traitors as friends. You have betrayed me by making me sleep where I'm miserable," Yuri declared.

"It's your turn," Rustik said.

"It's too hot to sleep there," Yuri insisted.

Igor sighed. "Someone has to be close to be sure the heater vents correctly and that sparks don't fly out into the tent."

"I know," Yuri was frustrated.

"It's your turn so do your best," Igor declared. The issue was solved as far as he was concerned.

"My jacket! It's burned now!" Yuri was angry at the mishap. His jacket had caught a spark from the heater and burned.

Sasha models Yuri Doroschenko's burned jacket.

Depending on their needs, they wore a variety of clothing: shirts, sweaters, layers of pants, and woolen or cotton socks. In the daytime, they wore boots and unlike modern skies, their boot strapped onto their skies; they wore their boots for skiing and hiking. At night inside the tent, they wore softer, felt boots. If during the night one of them needed to urinate, he or she often would go without a coat, brave the cold, and wore only socks or their felt boots.

Igor Dyatlov designed the group's tent. He also designed the heater's vent can be seen in the above photograph.

8

1.29.59

January 29, 1959

The tourists skied along the Auspiya River. It was -13 C or 6 degrees Fahrenheit.

A trail made by a Mansi hunter was visible. Zina noted: *"Along the Auspiya, Mansi have passed. A trail is visible, grooves, a path is visible. We often see Mansi signs on the trail. I wonder what they write about? Now the Mansi trail goes south."* There were many signs of the hunter, and the group followed his path because it was easier to ski on a broken trail. They took turns being the leader and plowing through the snow so that the others could ski easier.

An unsigned diary entry explains, *"Today as yesterday, we are following the path of Mansi. Sometimes Mansi writings appear on trees. In general, all sorts of obscure mysterious characters. There is a slogan for our campaign, "In a country of mysterious signs." If we knew these letters, it would be possible, without any doubt, to go down the path, confident that it would lead us to the right place. Here the trail takes us to the shores of the river. We lose track. In the future, the trail follows the left bank of Auspii (sic) River, but the team of deer crossed the river, and we are going through the woods. At the first opportunity, we will turn back to the river. As it is easier to follow it. At approximately 2 pm we stop for a lunch. Dried meat, guest crackers, sugar, garlic, coffee, stocked in the morning - that's our lunch. Good mood."*

Mansi record of a hunt: The three slashes at the top represent that there were three hunters on the trip. The second mark is the family symbol. The second set of three slashes represents how many animals were involved.
The date is 1958.

When they stopped for the night, Zina and Yuri gathered and sawed firewood. It was a chance to talk.

"You were sweet to lend me your mittens," Zina told him.

He ran a hand through his hair and replaced his hat. "I care."

"I'm surprised," Zina admitted.

"When I care, it is not for every girl."

Zina blurted, "I saw you talking, alone with that girl from the other group when we were on the train."

"And you were talking alone with Igor," Yuri shrugged. "You are warm and exciting, and everyone, especially men, are drawn to you. You are always busy with those who want to get close to you."

Zina wasn't sure if she were sad or frustrated. She had many male friends. "They don't matter."

"Igor matters."

Zina didn't respond. That was true, but….

"Sasha was right. People shouldn't kiss everyone to try to find the right one. People should kiss the right one because they are *right. The one.*" Yuri was adamant.

He was like her. It was all or nothing, and while she had dated him, she had spent time with male friends and been flattered by men who chased after her.

"I should wait for the right kiss," Zina said, strangely shy.

"A good kiss," Yuri grinned, "that is something we should have talked about when we dated."

"I wasn't dedicated enough then," Zina admitted. "I didn't know what we had and didn't appreciate it as I should."

"You need more kisses," Yuri teased her.

She blushed as he flirted.

Rustik, listening sometimes to the conversation, laughed.

In her journal Zina wrote about Yuri: *We talked about the past. Such a flirt.*

Igor Dyatlov remained calm, but he was affected by the fact that Zina and Yuri were once again getting close; he only showed his discomfort when he wrote in his journal where he kept a picture of Zina. He brooded over the photo but forced himself to concentrate on the summit and the goal of the group.

1.30.59

January 30, 1959

Inside the tent, the heater provided heat that was soothing and caused everyone to sleep later than expected. Sasha and Kolya were supposed to wake the others to get an early start, but they were so warm and cozy that they slept longer, causing the group to have a late start.

Igor was not amused.

"It feels so nice in here," Sasha attempted to excuse their behavior.

"I couldn't argue his plan," Kolya added, causing Sasha to frown.

Sasha shook his head. It had been Koyla's idea to sleep longer. "It wasn't me."

"You're both to blame," Igor said. "This is two mornings in a row you've slowed us."

Zina laughed. "And they should both be punished. Extra chores!"

The others agreed.

Sasha gave Kolya a dirty look and grumbled an obscenity.

"At least we got the extra sleep," Kolya responded, laughing. It was impossible for him to have a bad mood.

Georgy smirked. "Next time, I want in on the plan. I can always use extra sleep."

"No next time," Igor pretended to be angry, but everyone, including him, laughed.

Once awake and travelling again, the tourists skied alongside the Auspiya River but couldn't ski directly on the river since the warmer weather had made it unsafe. The clear skies allowed sunburns, and the wind caused windburn.

"It's as if an airplane is taking off," Igor complained. The wind was warm and strong.

Georgy laughed. "But here, as soon as you say that, it all changes."

For a while, the group made up lost time, but then, as is common in the Urals, just as Georgy predicted, the weather changed. Clouds filled the skies. A west wind blew so strongly that it caused the snow on the trees to fill the air as if it were a snowstorm; in addition, it began to snow. It grew colder. Thinning with the altitude, the tree line offered less protection.

At 2:00, they stopped to eat dried meat, garlic, crackers, and coffee with sugar. It was an easy lunch to eat quickly and provided quick energy and long-lasting energy.

They were behind schedule, had veered off course, and had lost the Mansi trail.

The tourists felt the effects when they neared a 10,000-foot altitude. At that level, anxiety, confusion, and some nausea could be present, but the group thought they felt fine; however, they knew they were exhausted. To their disbelief, they made several wrong turns on the slopes and passes.

Instead of continuing, they backtracked two hundred meters or 218 yards because they need a wooded area to build their cache for extra supplies. It was 5:00 PM.

After finding a place to camp where there was plenty of firewood, the tourists stopped for the night. Despite their exhaustion, there was a rule that chores had to be completed before relaxing. A fire was built, and Lyuda sat down to warm herself. The wood was damp and burned poorly.

"The tent needs mending. Zina did it last," Kolya told Lyuda.

"Then mend it. I want to rest for a few minutes. You caused the delays, so you do it."

"It's your turn," Kolya said. He quickly changed out of his wet shirt and felt better once he was dry; the cold wasn't quite as bad. Lyuda hadn't gotten up from her seat next to the fire, so he took his journal and wrote for a few minutes. He thought Lyuda was joking around.

Semyon wondered what was happening. "Are you not going to do the mending?" He dug snow away from the fire so the flames wouldn't melt the snow and put itself out.

"I have already said that I'm tired and I'm cold. Kolya and Sasha can do the extra chores since they caused the delay. If we keep putting off making the cache for supplies and failing to gain ground, we'll never summit on time."

Georgy shrugged. "We'll make it. Tomorrow might be easier." He refused to think failure was an option; it wasn't for him.

Zina agreed. "We'll build the cache tomorrow."

"We were supposed to build it today," Lyuda snapped. She was so tired and worried that they would turn back before reaching the summit. She might not even get her level 3 certification. Her frustration boiled over.

Igor adjusted a rope for the tent. He called to the rest, not shouting. Yet. "Someone mend the tent. Rules are rules."

Rustik was less polite. "Just mend the tent!"

"I'll do it," Kolya found the repair kit and took out a needle. He didn't want Lyuda to become angrier.

Semyon reached his hand out and said, "Give me a needle. I'll help."

"You can all do it." Lyuda held back tears and went to the tent where she crawled inside. She was aware that she was acting silly, but now that she was embarrassed and ashamed of herself, she needed time to calm herself before she apologized.

"Guess what? It's my birthday. Come wish me a good day, Lyuda," Sasha called to her.

She didn't answer.

Sasha was too embarrassed to admit he had said that to try to get Lyuda in a better mood, but it wasn't his birthday. Zina got excited and hugged him, and the men wished him the best. They gave him a tangerine to celebrate; he was so touched by their generosity and kindness that he almost cried. Because he didn't want to be selfish, he divided the fruit among the eight of them.

Zina last wrote:

30.2.59 We go on Auspiya. Cold Mansi trail ended. Pine forest. There was sun in the morning, now is cold. All day long we walked along Auspiya. Will spend the night on a Mansi trail. Kolya didn't get to be a watchman so me and Rustik will stay on duty today. Burned mittens and Yurda's second quilted jacket. He cursed a lot. Today, probably, we will build a storage. The brighter, the greater diaphragm number, if the diaphragm is lower, there will be less light on the film, the shutter speed is longer. Aperture – closed. Rempel.

It was -26 C or -15 F.

In the tent, they ate supper, and Lyuda felt more sociable, so she decided that maybe she was just very hungry when she showed her temper to the rest and refused to do her chores. To make up, she was more cheerful and took charge, doing more of the work of laying out the blankets, organizing, and stacking their boots to the side.

Zina and Rustik watched the heater to make sure it stayed safe after Kolya finished checking it and burning his mittens. Disgusted, he took them off and tossed them to Georgy who laughed the hardest. Georgy shoved the ruined mittens into his pants pockets and fell asleep chuckling.

Relationships have been tested, but nothing serious has happened. Everyone remains good friends, even Semyon, the new-comer.

There is nothing yet that has occurred to cause the tragedy that is about forty-eight hours away, yet, if the tragedy were to be compared to a storm, the group has ignored the barometric changes. They are in no state to avoid the storm and will rush into harm's way.

It's important to look closely at the last photograph taken of Igor Dyatlov. His eyes are blank: no life or light left

*Author's note: At this point, Dyatlov is aware that they are behind schedule, the weather is not improving, and everyone in the group is tired. He is as short-tempered as some of the others, and several times, each of them has made poor choices or poor suggestions of ideas. They are irritated by the conditions and by the fear of not making the summit.

1.31.59

January 31, 1959

The wind blew from the west, and it was -24 C or -11 F. Snow fell from the trees, blown by the wind and results comparable to trying to ski in a blizzard.

They deviated from the travel plans and planned to summit from a slightly different place. If they moved to a hill that had trees, they could build a good fire, but Igor made a critical decision.

As they skied, they took turns and broke the trail for the others. The leader took off his backpack, broke the trail through the snow, sometimes having to step sideways up a tough elevation, and made a path for about fifteen minutes. Then that person trudged back to his backpack, put it on, rested for ten minutes, and then hurried to catch up to the group. In this way, the trail was always broken for the other eight skiers, and each did a part of the work. It was effective and a smart plan, but exhausting.

Some competed to see who could make the best path in the least amount of time and who could keep up the hard work the longest. Rustik did his best, but Kolya and Igor almost bested him.

They moved about one mile per hour in this way which was a third of their usual speed. Their original plan was to make a cache on Hill 663, then to go to Hill 805, and then summit Mount Otorten. Instead, Igor changed the plan, and they headed toward Hill 805 without the stop to cache supplies and lighten their load. From Hill 805 to the summit was eleven miles of easy travel. He wanted to make it to Hill 611 which was a very easy downhill trip and only a few miles from Hill 805. Hill 611 was a lofty goal but one that would be the best.

Had they made it, their lives would have been spared.

But at 4:00, Igor realized that because of their slow progress, they'd never make it to the top of Hill 805, much less to Hill 611 where there was firewood. Already the trees were sparse and damp. The good spruces were behind them.

No one had enough energy to ski in the dark. It was too windy and cold to go on.

Igor made another critical decision. He turned the group back, south, to Hill 663 where they would have firewood, the cover and protection of the trees, and a good place to build the cache. It was too late to build the cache (labaz) that night; they were too exhausted, and the visibility was poor.

"We're too far behind schedule," Semyon told Igor.

Igor nodded. "But we need the firewood and the cache."

"If we make it to 805 and then to 611, we'll have firewood for the night, and that isn't very far," Georgy added. "We can do that tomorrow."

"That won't help us make up the time," Sasha said. "It's too short of a route."

"Then we'll bypass 611." Igor shrugged.

"Igor, we'll be without firewood or protection." Sasha was shocked.

Igor Dyatlov smiled, but there was no mirth in his eyes. "We'll take the heater." The little stove carried its own firewood inside. It provided enough warmth for them to camp anywhere and stay comfortable. "We're going between the hills to save time. We can make up six to eight hours tomorrow."

"I'll be glad to help chart the course," Semyon said.

"Thanks. We're going to be fine." Igor found that he respected Semyon and decided that they would be friends.

Left corner: Igor Dyatlov's leadership and travel plans are questioned by Semyon (in center) while Sasha looks on. Georgy takes the photo.

Igor wrote in the journal: *Tired and exhausted, we started the preparations for the night. Not enough firewood. Frail damp firs. We started fire with logs, too tired to dig a fire pit. We had supper right in the tent. It's warm. It is hard to imagine such a comfort somewhere on the ridge, with a piercing wind hundreds of kilometers away from human settlements.*

A firepit was best, but it required digging down through four to six feet of snow and building the fire on the ground. Since they were too tired to cut much firewood, they just lay logs on the snow and built the fire; everything was wet.

As soon as the tent was up, Yuri and Zina, a perfect team, put the heater together which was a long process because the vents had to be fitted perfectly. It was worth it because it made the tent cozy. As soon as their food was warmed, they retreated to the tent to have their supper, to relax, and rest.

"Thank you for helping me with the blankets and with gathering the wood, Semyon," Lyuda said. He had worked tirelessly to help her with all of her chores. Her smile was warm.

"Glad to help," Semyon grinned happily.

"I know what we can do." Zina took out her pencil and paper. "Everyone would love to hear of our adventures. We need a newspaper with headlines that grip readers."

She wrote: *The Evening Otorten, February 1, 1959, Issue 1.*

"Now what?" Igor was amused.

"Now you tell me what headlines we should have." Zine looked around expectantly.

Yuri spoke up first. "*A team of radio technicians including Comrades Doroshenko and Kolmogorova set a new world record for portable stove assembly: one hour, two minutes, and twenty-seven point four seconds.* That's for sports news."

Zina squealed with pleasure and excitement. "That's perfect." She wrote quickly.

"*Increased birthrate among tourists,*" Georgy said, grinning.

"Georgy!" Lyuda tossed a mitten at him.

"*Seminars about love and tourism to be held in the tent and are taught by Dr. Thibeaux and post doctorate of love science, Dubinina,*" Zina announced.

Kolya nodded happily. "I am a professor of love? That's fantastic. That should really happen."

"You wish," Georgy smirked. "What do you know about love?"

"I'm a professor and I don't have to explain the intricacies."

"As an editorial, add this: *Can nine tourists get by with one heater and one blanket*?" Igor said. "Of course, they can. My heater works to keep us warm and comfortable."

"That's so smart. It's a wonderful headline," Zina said. "But I'm glad we have more than one blanket."

"Science. *In recent years, there has been a heated debate about the existence of yetis. According to recent reports, yeti lives in the Northern Urals near the Otorten Mountains. The snowman is real.*" Kolya grinned.

Everyone chuckled, and Kolya stood, hunched over as he pretended to be a yeti. He growled. Georgy, not to be outdone, mimicked the yeti impression, making everyone laugh harder.

"Technical. *Tourist sledge. Good while riding on the train, by car, and on horseback. Not recommended for freight transportation on snow. For further information contact Chief Constructor Kolevatov.*" Sasha added his headline.

"I have several, but I'm about to fall asleep," Rustik said. "Most are about my athletic abilities."

"Of course, they are," Zina giggled.

"Can we add to this tomorrow night?" Semyon asked. He enjoyed the creativity. It was the most fun he had enjoyed with the group and felt as if he were a real member of the friends.

Zina nodded. She put the paper away. "if you enjoy the game, we can play again." She was pleased they liked her game.

Semyon nodded. "I love it. It exercises my mind."

"And it's funny," Kolya added.

"Lyuda and I can set a record for gathering firewood for the sports section," Semyon said. "And maybe I can carry more weight to get a headline."

"I'll carry the most and get a better headline," Lyuda warned Semyon, but she smiled warmly.

"Rustik Slobodin runs up the mountain in one hour to set a new world record," Rustik said.

"Comedian Georgy Krivo summits mountain in twelve minutes."

Kolya looked at Georgy and rolled his eyes. "Attractive, brilliant, comedian Kolya Tibo summits mountain. Time doesn't matter at all."

Hilarity erupted.

"Dr. Igor Dyatlov earns his level 10 certification." Igor puffed out his chest.

Zina burst into peals of laughter. "Level 10? Why not 20? What a headline *that* is."

"Sasha tosses eight tourists into the heater to keep warm and to make them be quiet so he can sleep."

Zina blinked and cocked her head, "Too long."

Slowly, the voices faded as one by one the tourists fell asleep. Despite the stress that Igor felt, the game that Zina encouraged them to play relaxed the tourists, made them laugh, and boosted moral.

They slept warmly.

*Author's note: In side by side comparisons. The journals contain discrepancies. Some wrote in the evenings; some wrote when they rested. Often, events were recorded but happened days before. In addition, all the original ten had diaries, and there was also an official group journal that was to be turned in to the university. That is eleven journals. The government released only six, and one belonged to Yuri Yudin who was not even on the slopes; therefore, half of the journals are unavailable to compare notes. My interpretation is based on logic, the photos, and careful comparisons, but it is possible the sequence of events was slightly different.

Other than the change in route that Igor Dyatlov made, the actions of the group are of minor importance.

The change in route was serious, and I have presented it factually.

Even though it was a bold choice that Igor made, the change should have worked out. Had other elements not interfered, despite the change, the tourists would have summited. However, the decision to travel a different course and then the subsequent choice of a camp, and the other facets of imperfect storm sentenced the Dyatlov Nine to death.

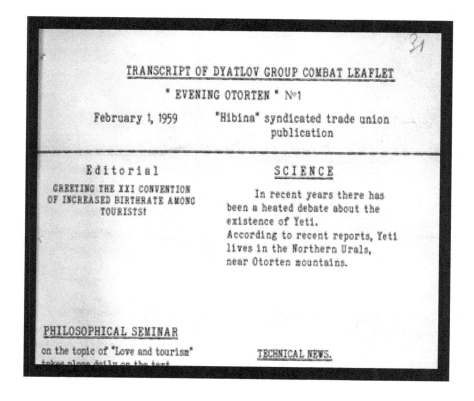

31

TRANSCRIPT OF DYATLOV GROUP COMBAT LEAFLET

" EVENING OTORTEN " №1

February 1, 1959   "Hibina" syndicated trade union
                                                    publication

Editorial

GREETING THE XXI CONVENTION
OF INCREASED BIRTHRATE AMONG
TOURISTS!

SCIENCE

In recent years there has been a heated debate about the existence of Yeti.
According to recent reports, Yeti lives in the Northern Urals, near Otorten mountains.

PHILOSOPHICAL SEMINAR

on the topic of "Love and tourism"
takes place daily in the tent

TECHNICAL NEWS.

Some of the ravines were very deep. As the water froze and snow covered the bottoms, it became difficult to see the ravines.

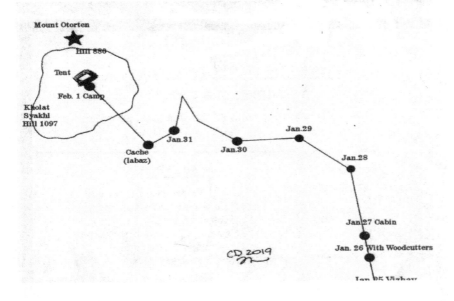

Author's Map: Travels from January 25 in Vezhay to campsite in January 31, 1959. On February 1, the tourists descended the slope to a wooded area to build the labaz (cache) and then ascended to Kholat Syakhl to build their final camp.

Part 11

1

2.1.1959 Day

February 1, 1959

Still exhausted, the group slept later than usual, but no one was to blame; they all wanted more rest. The higher the altitude, the more difficult it is to sleep well, but the body requires more rest. As the body wears down, it becomes easier to get cold, hypothermia sets in.

Although the altitude was not extreme, combined with the freezing temperatures, wind, and constant work skiing, the tourists were not in good physical health; worrying about the summit affected their mental health.

When they were dressed warmly and ready to work, they built a cache for extra supplies to lighten their loads in preparation for the summit. Cutting the wood and the building scraped their hands, and some of the springy branches snapped against their faces, causing scratches. They worked slowly.

The platform was positioned off the ground and was very secure so that after the summit, they could ski around and back down to the *labaz* to collect the stashed supplies. Once the cache *(labaz)* was finished, they filled it with everything that was unneeded, too heavy, or bulky. Items they left included extra food, a first aid kit, their extra skis, batteries, a pair of boots with socks, and the mandolin.

"We need to add the heater to the *labaz*," Rustik said. He wondered why Igor forgot.

Igor shook his head. "Last night we were warm and slept better. It was comfortable. We'll carry it with us since there won't be firewood available higher on the mountain."

"Of course, there will be wood. 611 is wooded." Rustik was confused.

"From here, we'll go between 805 and 1079."

Semyon nodded. "We're too far behind, and we should bypass 611. It'll be faster."

Georgy wiped sweat from his face. He was soaked in sweat from the work they had done. "That's not far."

"Faster?" Rustik was becoming angry, especially since Semyon had inserted himself into a major change of plans. "It's cold. The wind is maddening. We're late getting started since we had to build the *labaz*. It only makes sense to go to 611 where there is wood, and it's as far as we can travel today in these conditions." Even as he said it, he wondered if he were right. It wouldn't add much to their distance.

"We'll make better time this way," Semyon said.

"I didn't ask you," Rustik said, taking umbrage. If anyone were second in command, it was Rustik. "Igor, we have to go to 611. What are you thinking?"

"We'll be less than eleven miles from the summit this way. Ten. We can sleep warmly with the heater, get a good night's rest, and make the summit tomorrow."

"That's going to put us without firewood. We're getting such a late start, too." Rustik felt that Igor wasn't listening to him.

"Most of it is easy. The pass will be the most difficult, and we can sidestep that small part since we have a lighter load. Why are you questioning such a simple, smart change in plans?" Igor really questioned why Rustik was questioning *him*, the leader. Semyon was on board with the plan. Sasha and Georgy didn't complain. The others were quiet. Only Rustik was cocky enough to suggest this was a mistake.

It might be.

Igor knew that it was very cold, close to -30 C or -22 F. The winds were mercilessly strong. The visibility was low. But they had to do this. Men and women of Soviet Russia defined themselves by facing extremes and overcoming their personal doubts. The trip was for a level 3 certification and needed to be tough so that each member of the group would learn to make hard choices and to execute changes in plans.

They didn't have to add it to the group's diary, either. No one needed to know that they had to change strategies.

And his plan would make up some of the time they had lost because they had not built the *labaz* sooner and at a higher elevation. That was a mistake, and he refused to make another.

"That's three hundred yards to sidestep when we are exhausted," Rustik said.

"You feel I am a poor leader incapable of wise decisions, now? Have I failed?" Igor asked.

Rustik looked at the ground, and then at Igor. They had been friends far too long for them to argue. Igor was the leader and deserved respect; Rustik admitted that aloud. He apologized sincerely. He had over-stepped the boundaries; a leader had to be trusted. He trusted Igor.

Igor, as a leader, knew that he had over-reacted and regretted being harsh. A good leader didn't allow emotions to take over good sense. He hugged Rustik. "Brother."

The entire incident was forgotten.

Semyon set the course.

The tourists headed toward the summit.

And death.

The fight wasn't important; however, the change in plans was. The alternate plan added power to the storm of tragedy that was coming. It wasn't too late if nothing else fueled the storm....

2

The Storm Begins

2.1.1959 Night

Despite their stamina and determination, the hikers could not keep going; they were too fatigued. They had barely covered three miles at the most because the weather was far worse than before. Not only was it extremely cold, but also the wind blew hard and relentlessly. The sweat chilled them as they cooled down, and even their underclothing was damp and cold against their skin.

The tent site was dug just below the peak of the hill for the "walls" that offered some protection from the west wind. It was difficult work and made harder by the fact that they had to also dig out a level area for the tent to rest on. Exhausted and in the miserable conditions, they had to struggle to do the work.

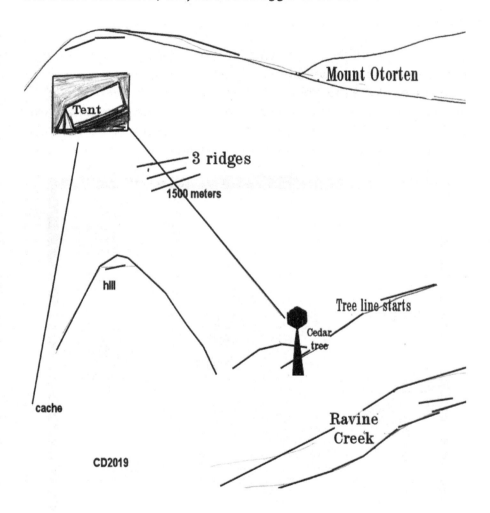

With night approaching, Igor decided to camp slightly below the peak, not only for wind protection, but also because the winds divided forces around the hill; the winds missed the tent area for the most part. Igor made this decision with a lot of thought. Alternately, they could try for Hill 611 where there was the cover of trees and firewood, but they were very tired and cold. The compass would help them arrive there even if there were a white out, but they would have to travel after dark. Physically, although in excellent condition, that was possibly beyond their endurance.

The second choice was to ski back to the *labaz* where there were trees to block the wind and there was available firewood. That would demoralize the tourists because they would lose an entire day of work and have to ski back to the same spot again the next day. Again, they were cold and fatigued, and their destination would be in sight as a morale booster.

After considering all the choices, setting up the tent where they were in daylight, and getting sleep and a fresh start was the best idea. Losing ground or going any farther was simply not the right plan. As an experienced leader, Igor used all his knowledge and skills to make the call.

"Maybe we should sing while we work, Zina," Georgy suggested.

She frowned but then smiled. "Yes, but my lips are too cold to try."

Lyuda packed the snow firm where the tent would lie. It would be positioned over most of their skies to provide a platform and protection against the cold.

"Thanks," Rustik told Igor as his friend handed him another bucket of snow to toss to the side. As a team, the two worked tirelessly to remove the snow that the others dug away. The earlier argument was long forgotten, and they joked and tried to work the hardest, to encourage the others.

Sasha and Semyon dug furiously, trying to make plenty of room for the large tent that could, in a pinch, sleep up to twelve people. Sasha told the other man, "I'm glad you joined us, Semyon. You're a hard worker and have a positive personality. It's as if you've always been a part of our little family."

Semyon was touched. He had felt increasingly welcomed but hearing the words made him smile. Sasha was often reserved, so to hear that from him was spirit-lifting. Sasha was very protective of the group's members, and Semyon felt that Sasha was now protective of him as well. Semyon was so elated that he worked harder.

"Maybe I can get some tobacco from you sometime," Semyon said.

"You smoke a pipe?" Sasha asked. He was shivering but able to smile even though it was a sort of grimace.

Semyon shrugged. "I can start." He smiled and felt good.

Until Kolya tossed a snowball at his back.

"What was that for?" Semyon spun around and asked, amused.

Kolya grinned, "Be happy that I didn't drop it down your back. You and Sasha are digging out more snow than I can carry away." He pretended that his bucket weighed a lot and that it was too heavy to carry.

"Work harder," Sasha insisted.

"I'll get you, next," Koyla laughed as he warned Sasha. He carried the bucket to the side and dumped the contents.

Yuri and Zina unfolded the tent in preparation of setting it up as soon as the pad was finished. "You know what might warm your lips for singing…."

Zina blushed, despite her cold face. "You're impossible. Is this the way you win me back?"

"I tried once before. Only when you are ready to be won can I succeed. But why do you want a poor boy?" Yuri pretended to pout.

Zina felt a rush of affection. "Because we'll both soon have good jobs and we won't be poor. Neither of us, Yurda." She was aware that when they returned home, there was now a chance that she would have to tell Igor they couldn't date anymore. Or she might tell Yuri that she couldn't take another chance with him.

Both men shared her interests, were big-hearted, intelligent, brave, and kind, and either would make a fine husband. Her heart was torn, but only Lyuda knew how seriously Zina was thinking about the situation. Lyuda didn't know what advice she could offer; she liked both Igor and Yuri tremendously, and although she hated that Zina was emotionally confused, the situation was one to envy: two great men to choose from.

Yuri told Zina, "Maybe we can set a new world record tonight for getting warm. I mean setting up our heater." He was so cold his teeth chattered.

Zina giggled. Her choice was becoming clearer.

Georgy handed Lyuda Igor's Chinese flashlight; it was getting dark fast as a worse storm approached. He was more than shivering; he was shaking.

With his help, the rest erected the tent, tied the ropes to skies to keep the top taut, tossed the backpacks inside, and crawled in as night descended; they fell on the tent's floor, almost too cold and too tired to move.

Outside, the wind increased, starting to blow around the sides of the hill.

3

Inside the Tent

"Once we get the heater going, we'll be warm." Igor didn't move yet. He was hungry and they would have a mostly cold meal with their coffee or tea and meat warmed with the heater. He was hungry, yes, but he was also a bit nauseated which was a strange combination. The nausea passed, and he felt fine.

"Let me get everything organized," Lyuda said. She took their foodstuff and set it aside with the other cooking equipment. She motioned Sasha and Georgy to line their boots up. Their tent shoes, which they would put on as soon as they had the energy, went to one side of the tent. The axe, flask, and a few other supplies went at the front, and a bucket and the heater went close to the opening.

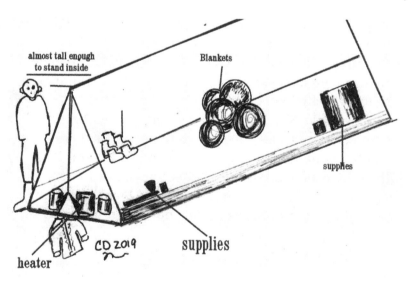

...la and Zina spread out the backpacks and jackets ...lankets, Koyla pulled off his boots and slipped on ...; with wool socks used as insoles and his wool ...d a sheepskin jacket; he was still very cold. His ...were worn out but comfortable. Over his underwear he wore blue cotton pants and warm woolen pants with the cuffs fastened securely.

"Are you that cold, Koyla?" Rustik teased.

"No. I'm not very cold at all. I'm all covered up," Koyla responded, witty as usual. His pale green eyes twinkled. He was almost giddy. "Like you are."

Rustik laughed. He wore an undershirt, a black and red checked shirt with his pocket secured by a safety pin so his passport stayed safe, a blue knitted shirt, and a sweat shirt. Over his underwear, he wore a pair of grey fleece long johns and a pair of sports pants. He wore two pairs of cotton socks and two pairs of woolen socks. He added another watch to his arm because he was in charge of getting everyone up in the morning. Distracted and in no rush, he put on one felt boot but paused to listen to the wind.

The storm was almost directly over them, and it screamed like a woman and moaned like an old man. It rumbled. Thunder started to explode with loud bangs.

Lyuda was cold. She wore a yellow shirt, a sweater, tights, pants, and two pairs of socks. She needed to dry some of her clothing next to the heater but didn't ask anyone else for more warm clothing. She almost reached for her boots, but waited, too tired to move anymore. She wrapped one of the blankets around her; she needed to spread all the blankets out but trembled as she listened to the thunder and wind.

"The storm is getting worse. If the wind keeps increasing, it could blow the tent and us right off the slope," Sasha said. He wore long underwear over his other underwear, and khaki pants on his lower body; on top he wore an undershirt, a checked shirt, a ragged grey sweater, and a brown fleece sweater. On his feet were brown cotton socks, and he was ready to get his feet in his tent shoes. He didn't put them on because he listened to the storm, as mesmerized as everyone else.

Zina thought she would never get warm; she and Yuri needed to get the stove set up. Everyone laughed at her, but she wore a red wool hat over a red knitted cap. Over her underwear, she wore two pairs of sports pants. To warm her core, she wore a blue knitted shirt, a red sweater, a checked shirt, and a blue sweater. She mis-matched her socks: one was blue wool, and the other was brown. The noise of the storm made her anxious, and she felt disinterested in her chore. Apathy ruled at 10,000 feet.

Georgy wore a pair of brown socks, a sleeveless undershirt, checked shirt, swim trunks, and long underwear. He felt too warm despite the freezing temperatures. He had no desire to put on his tent boots; he was far too warm, which was confusing. His clothing felt clammy from his sweat; he should have worked less ferociously.

Yuri was miserable in a blue undershirt, a red and blue checked shirt, and a sleeveless green vest. Over his underwear, he wore long underwear and blue sateen pants. Over brown wool socks, he wore white cotton socks, but felt warm, but damp. Damp-warm was uncomfortable. He needed to change into dry clothing as soon as possible. He said, "We might not be safe here even with the snow walls we made around the tent. The wind is brutal."

The noise was a strong grumble, and it started to roar.

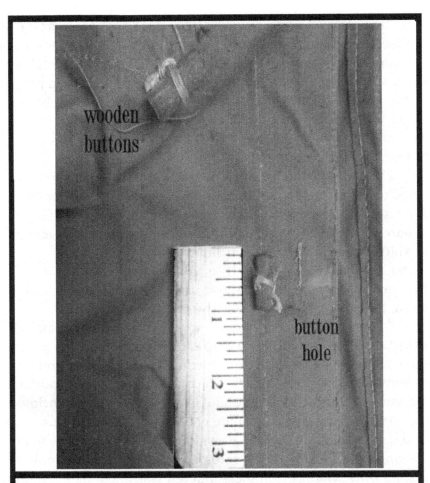

(ND 2019) Example of the tent's wooden buttons and button holes.

Igor sat up straight, alert to the intensity of the storm. It was far worse than he had anticipated and had already blown snow against the tent opening. Although they buttoned it up tightly, the last few buttons holes at the bottom were open to allow them to go out to urinate when needed, and his coat, stuffed into the tent's opening, blocked the worst of the wind gusts, but their tent was in danger. He held the flashlight, so they had light and was able to discern growing concern among his friends.

He wore a blue undershirt, a blue and red checked shirt, and a green knitted, sleeveless vest. Over underwear, he had blue sateen pants over long underwear, and two pairs of brown woolen socks.

Each needed to add dry clothing and layers and put on the felt tent shoes.

They needed to assemble the heater.

And to eat.

They needed to finish their chores and write in the group journal, yet they didn't. They only listened to the worsening storm, wondering if they were about to be blown down the slope.

"Sorry. I need to go outside. I'll be quick and try to keep the gusts from coming into the tent." Semyon was tough as he braved the cold to walk out to relieve himself, taking his camera to get some shots of the magnificent lightning show over the hill. The flashes were dramatic, but the thunder was almost deafening and growing louder. Like the explosion of bombs or concentrated gunfire.

It was brutally cold, and he was glad he had his boots.

Odd.

The sounds were like those he had heard when fighting in the war on the front line.

Koyla and Georgy had illegal Finnish knives; Sasha had permission from the police to carry one, and several of the men carried pocket knives. Semyon liked the others, and he trusted them, but he kept his own Finnish knife hidden. There was no reason to show it off, but because he was former military, he was trained to carry something for protection. His knife was in his deepest pocket.

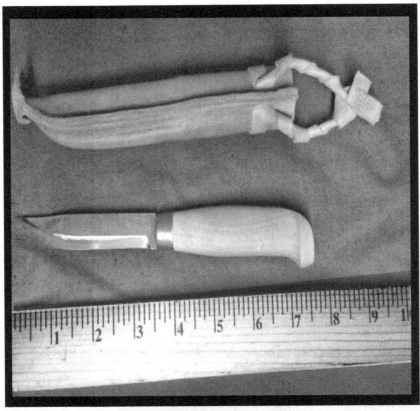

(ND2019) Finnish knife and sheath.

On his head was a black fur hat with ear flaps and a red, woolen cap. He had a warm wool scarf that was brown and blue. On his upper body he wore two cotton undershirts, a thick black sweater, and a heavy jacket. Lower, he wore underwear, cotton trunks, trousers with an elastic waist band, and ski pants. He wore two socks on one foot, and, on the other foot, he wore one, but inside his felt boots were wool socks used as insoles.

In ordinary conditions, he would have been warm and comfortable, but the conditions were not usual. He was cold and miserable, and the claps of thunder reminded him of the war. They became louder.

Semyon thought he was back in the war; he felt disoriented and his hair stood on end. Was that a louder noise just behind the cacophony of the thunder?

At the same time, the storm changed. The noise became as loud as a freight train. A tornado was sweeping down the upper slopes and would toss the tent and all the travelers across the slope and likely injure them severely, probably kill them. Semyon had to save the group that he had come to love as family.

There was no time to waste.

He ran to the tent.

*Author's note: Paradoxical undressing occurs when a person is cold but flushes heat and feels overly warm; the result is that, even in poor conditions, some remove clothing or dress in less clothing than what is needed.

* They were at 10,00 feet and felt the beginnings of slight *hypoxia*.

* Author's note: Considering the weather conditions and the physical state of the group, Igor's decision about where to camp the night of February 1 was actually the best choice that he had. The other posibilities would have appealed to a less savvy leader, but Igor knew that; above all, he had to boost morale by not losing ground and by having their summit in sight. Psychologically, he was correct. Travelling at night for several hours and then erecting a tent would have been almost impossible. He knew all this. Although camping where they did ultimatly contributed greatly to the tragedy, in no way did Igor make a mistake and a bad choice; he did the best he could, given the curcumstances that had maligned against them. Nature dealt the first blow.

4

Panic

"Get out," Semyon yelled. "Get out. You'll blow away. Now. Move!" His head ached and he felt anxious. In fact, he felt terrified. "Get out."

Inside the tent, the tourists heard the tornado and knew that if the wind, caught the tent, they would be blown down the slope, their bones broken and crushed. Igor's head snapped up as he listened to the increasing noise; his heart raced. "Move."

Rustik, next to the doorway, forced himself through the small opening, knowing he might not have time to unbutton the flaps. The wooden buttons were too difficult to push through the button holes, especially when someone had cold fingers. That was why they just left a few buttons undone so that it was easy to slide through to go outside to urinate. It wasn't a large enough opening to rush through. Not for eight people. He pushed the snow away and crawled, pulling himself to his feet, feeling the noise vibrating within his bones.

Georgy was right behind him, but the opening was small, the snow piled high, and it took too long to exit. He hurried, crawled on hands and knees, but he wasn't fast enough for those who were yelling behind him.

Semyon yanked free his Finnish knife, dropped the sheath, and began to slash an opening. His first attempts were futile, too high, too small, ineffective. He quickly moved to the back of the tent and with all his strength cut a gash from top to bottom. "Get out. Hurry."

The noise grew louder, drowning his words.

Lyuda dashed through the opening as Igor held the sides so she could fit. As she hurried, she dropped the Chinese flashlight that she had been holding to add more light, if necessary in the tent, but had not turned it on, and it landed on the top of the tent. She didn't know where it was in the dark. She felt disoriented. "The light...."

"Leave it, Lyuda," Semyon shouted.

She ran to Georgy who hugged her. "What's happening?" she yelled into his ear.

"Just the wind and thunder. A storm. It's okay, Lyuda. Stay close to me." He kept one arm around her.

Yuri and Zina pulled themselves through the cut in the tent, yelling for the others to move faster. Zina thought the tent was moving. Yuri pulled her arm as she tried to grab a jacket, "No time. Come on."

Kolya crawled through the regular tent flaps last; Rustik pulled him along and to his feet, refusing to go to safety until everyone was out of the tent.

"Thanks."

"You're too slow," Rustik yelled to Kolya.

Semyon yanked Sasha through the opening he had made. Sasha almost fell but caught himself and hurried over to Georgy and Lyuda, mentally ticking off who was safe and who was still in the tent. Only seconds had passed, but he felt as if they were all moving slowly.

"Igor, come on. Get out of there," Sasha called.

Igor waited for the others to get free of the tent and to relative safety, then exited into the fury of the storm through the tent flaps, leaving behind the jacket that was right at the opening. There was no time to find the jacket in the dark. He motioned for them to get together; Rustik and Semyon helped. They formed a tight circle with their heads close together and their bodies hunched over. While Georgy protected Lyuda, Yuri kept an arm around Zina.

Everyone was out.

Igor yelled over the noise; it was slightly less thunder . "Tree line. Cover and fire. We can bivouac there."

"Stay calm. I have the flashlight," Georgy said.

"The trees? That's a mile away, Igor," Rustik protested. "We need to...."

"A mile is okay. Maybe it's a half mile. I don't know." Igor tried to make it seem less of a trek. The noise stayed thunderous, but the wind blew on both sides of them. So far, they were fortunate that they had camped just below the hill; it had saved them.

They were already walking away from the tent; it was almost too late to go back, and too dangerous. They needed lower ground. Semyon cursed the wind as they walked.

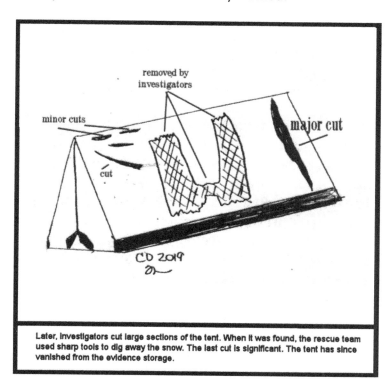

Later, investigators cut large sections of the tent. When it was found, the rescue team used sharp tools to dig away the snow. The last cut is significant. The tent has since vanished from the evidence storage.

em, the wind whipped around and dumped a large
he center of the tent, collapsing it. They walked

ıs underdressed and wore far less than the others.
....ʋarly bare. It was doubtful, in the snow and frigid
wind, that he would make it with his fingers and toes intact. He
feared frostbite and amputation, but he knew that his life was in
danger, too. He didn't say another word; he didn't want to be a
burden on the rest, but his feet started to ache before he walked
very far.

He was afraid.

"I dropped my flashlight…somewhere…where?" Lyuda
couldn't remember and she was terrified. An avalanche might be
set off by the storm's winds, and none of them would survive if that
occurred. It was one of her worst fears, being caught in an
avalanche. Her feet ached, too, and she resisted the urge to tell
anyone how cold she was.

"Walk faster," Igor ordered. "We have to get to the tree
line."

In the wind with snow falling and visibility limited and
because it was night, they couldn't see where they were going. The
flashlight didn't help much, and in their panicked state of mind, no
one thought about checking pockets for a compass. They didn't
have time to use a compass anyway. They had to get off the rise
and to a protected area or they would die.

In the confusion, some thought they were headed toward
the *labaz*. They were so afraid and shaken that they didn't recall
how far the tree line was exactly; only Rustik thought it was a mile
away, but maybe he was wrong. Thunder exploded again, and they
continued down the slope in an orderly manner, most walking in
sets of twos or threes. They wanted to run to safety. They wanted
to hurry down the slope, but the snow was deep, and walking was
difficult. Without visibility, no matter how terrified they were, they
had to move slowly. At any time, the tent and its contents could
blow into them, killing them.

"Keep going. I'll look around to see if we're going the right way," Koyla said. He did and was bewildered. The way to the tree line should be downhill from the tent, but he wasn't sure if it really was. It was confusing. They needed to angle downward.

"I should do it," Igor protested when Kolya reported.

Kolya shook his head. "I have boots, and besides, they need you to keep them going." He moved off to the side again and walked alone, trying to see where they were headed. Although he could only see a few yards in front of him and wished for moonlight, he tried his best. He saw nothing.

After a few minutes, he adjusted his course and angled back to the group. "Just keep going down the slope."

Behind them, the wind still roared and rushed down both sides of the peak. Had the peak not been there, the winds would have thrown them down the slope in a rush. It was a fortunate phenomenon. In certain circumstances, when people walk in the snow, there is a singularity that occurs with foot- prints. The body's weight compacts snow and makes it solid. When the wind blows away the loose, light snow, the footprints are left and look like columns. As the nine walked away from camp, their footprints were preserved. As the nine walked away from camp, their footprints were preserved.

Those without shoes left bare prints.

Their feet started to go numb. Lyuda lost her
balance and fell, leaving a handprint in the snow.

"My feet are so cold." She was never one to complain or to tell others that she was miserable, but her feet ached horribly, and she realized that almost everyone else was having the same pain. She was so scared for their feet that she almost cried.

"Come here," Rustik said. Without asking her, he picked Lyuda up in his arms to carry her. Although she protested and wiggled, he held tightly. "I'm perfectly capable of carrying you, and besides, I have boots." He didn't remind her that he had been listening to the storm, chilled by the eerie noise, and in his haste to leave the tent, he never put on his other boot.

Yuri and Georgy suffered; of the nine, they were the least warm with no shoes and only light shirts. Igor wasn't dressed much better.

"All we have to do is get to the tree line," Igor said over and over. "We can make a fire, and we'll be protected from the worst of the wind. "Keep moving. We have to be close, I'm sure. It can't be far."

And they did keep moving.

The first ridge was unexpected. They couldn't see the slight rise and the rocks beneath a thin layer of snow.

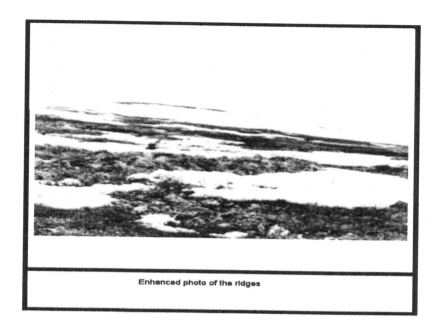

Enhanced photo of the ridges

Igor plummeted forward and caught himself on his knees, bruising and abrading them as well as his ankles. He scraped his hands. "Damn." For a few seconds, he was unsure if the pain were dulled by shock or freezing nerves or because he wasn't hurt badly. There was no time to consider his injuries because, before he could shout a warning, Yuri banged down the same set of rocks, yelling as he rolled.

"Yurda...." Zina struggled down the rocks to his side, bashing her side on a large rock; she would have a wide, large bruise on her back and side from the impact, but she didn't stop until she reached Yuri.

He lay on his back. His shins, upper thigh, arm, and chest were abraded and bruised, but he was so cold that he only moaned, more afraid of what he didn't feel than what he did. His hand was deeply cut, but he hardly felt that at all. "I'm okay, Zina. See? I'm fine." He struggled to his feet. Once upright, he wavered.

"You've cut yourself," Zina argued, worried.

Yuri was not stupid. He knew he was far too cold to go on much longer, and he was battered. He wanted nothing more than to go back to the tent, sit by the heater, and allow Zina to bandage his injuries. He wanted his warm clothing. For the sake of the others, he had to forgo the tent that could blow away and get to the tree line. He wasn't sure if he would make it that far; his feet were freezing.

His situation was serious, getting close to critical. For some reason, he had gotten pre-hypothermic while setting up the tent, just as George had, and then Yuri felt overly warm in the tent. He had never warmed up and was rapidly approaching deadly hypothermia.

Sasha slipped and bruised his left knee but got back to his feet at once. He refused to even wince; he had to be strong.

"Keep going. It isn't much farther," Igor lied. He had to get the group to safety. The high winds were dangerous, and the group needed protection. It was the only idea he had.

"It's too far," Lyuda said. "Yuri, Georgy, and you are not dressed for this. None of us are."

"Listen, the winds are too strong above and at the tent. We could be tossed off the slope. Semyon had to cut the tent to save us so it would allow only a little protection from the cold anyway," Igor explained.

"The heater...." Zina began. "We can put it together and get warm again."

Igor wanted to scream; no one understood the bigger picture. "It can be set up in a little over an hour in the best of circumstances. With the freezing temperature that the tent won't protect us from, it will take two or three times as long. We'd freeze."

"We'd have out jackets and blankets," Zina argued.

"The wind is blowing so hard that sparks would fly out of the heater and catch everything on fire or at least cause massive smoke and some burns. We're still talking about three hours, Zina." Igor rubbed his scraped hands and hoped to feel the pain; he didn't feel much.

"So? What now?"

"Zina, I told you. We go to the tree line, gather wood, and make a warm fire. It'll be faster than using the heater, and we'll be away from the wind."

"Okay. Okay. You're right, but I can't think right now," Zina said.

They carefully made their way over some rocks, and then Yuri stumbled on the second ridge, falling on his rear so hard that a large bruise formed. He cursed as once again, he had to get to his feet. His feet felt like numb blocks. When he met Georgy's eyes, he knew his friend was just as scared of having his own feet frozen.

Igor repeated his mantra, "We're getting close. We've been walking for over a half hour." What he forgot, didn't know, or chose to ignore was that they walked slowly in the snowstorm and blowing wind with freezing feet and that the nearest tree was 1500 meters (1640 yards) from where their tent was. They were only a third of the way toward their goal.

The third ridge would the worst for them.

Georgy fell first, injuring both shins and abrading his inner arms as he fell and slid feet first. He roared louder than the wind. Semyon and Sasha rushed to him and got him back on his feet.

Rustik fell second.

He first pushed Lyuda to the side to protect her, and she fell on her rear but was uninjured. Rustik was not as lucky. He tilted forward, unable to stop the direction he was falling. Hitting the ground headfirst, he smashed one side of his head against a sharp rock, rolled as he fell on the slope, and hit the other side of his skull. He didn't move.

"Rustik. Get up," Lyuda cried. She cared little for her own safety and scrambled to him as fast as possible. Kolya shadowed her and bent down to check Rustik at the same time Lyuda did.

"He's so still," Sasha said. "Is he okay?"

Rustik's eyes remained closed.

"He's unconscious. He's breathing." Kolya moved over slightly so Igor could confirm.

Igor patted Rustik's face, then patted him harder. Igor looked at the swelling and abrasions on Rustik's white, blank face. "Wake up, now. We have no time for this. Get up and walk. Come on."

Rustik's eyes opened, but he looked as if he didn't know where he was. Slowly he remembered rushing from the tent and the long walk in the cold, but he didn't remember falling even when Semyon explained that he had taken a nasty fall.

Sasha looked very worried.

Igor saw that both sides of Rustik's head looked raw, but there were no deep cuts or indentions. "Can you sit up?"

"I've been able to sit up since I was a small child," Rustik said, but Igor and Semyon helped him. Igor and Semyon traded glances and looked at the others; Rustik wasn't generally cheeky.

"How do you feel?"

"Like my head may explode with pain, but maybe it'll go as numb as the rest of my body."

"Let's get you on your feet," Semyon said, and he and Igor lifted Rustik. "How's that?"

Rustik swayed as dizziness hit him. He felt almost giddy. "I'm drunk."

"No, you just hurt your head. Can you walk?" Igor asked, worried.

"As I said, I've done so since I was a small child."

Igor and Semyon traded looks again. Besides a head injury, their friend was obviously showing signs of shock. They had to get to the tree line faster. They needed to make a fire and care for Rustik. Almost everyone had some injuries, and Igor wished for the first aid kit.

He wished for boots and a jacket.

He wished the wind and snow would stop.

He just wished.

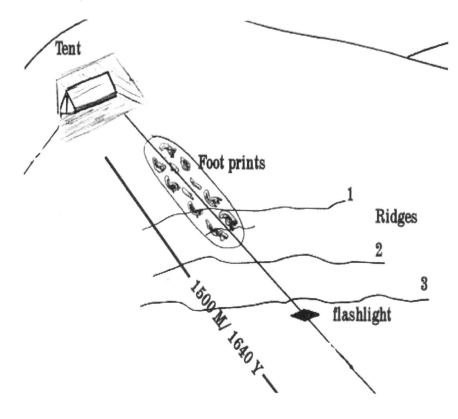

- Author's note: Only three Finnish knives were found in the tent. They were all in sheaths. Another empty sheath was found outside the tent's entrance but its owner was misidentified. *It is illogical to assume that Semyon, a war veteran, would not have had a Finnish knife as well. The investigators claimed that the cuts were made from within the tent, but forensics was very new at that time, and it's very flawed to imagine someone inside made the cuts and then exited with a knife but without proper clothing.

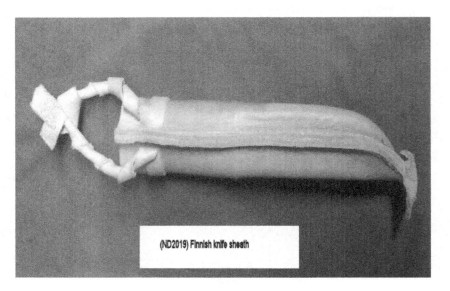

(ND2019) Finnish knife sheath

5

Rustem Vladimirovich Slobodin (Rustik)

Georgy dropped the flashlight. For a while, the light bulb had been dimming, but it finally went out, and they were left without any light.

Even with the storm and the ridges behind them, they should have travelled faster, but without light, the various injuries, and Rustik's head wound, they moved slowly. Sasha and Semyon stayed on both sides of Rustik to help him with balance. Cold, numb feet made it hard to keep walking, but at least it was downhill.

But the snow was deeper as the slope continued.

If they didn't get warm soon, they knew they would die.

Yuri said it first, "If we don't get to the trees soon and get a fire going, I won't make it."

"Yes, you will," Zina argued. She was determined to carry him on her back before allowing him to give up, lie down in the snow, and die. *Die.* The word was almost a word she never thought of. She didn't think of it in terms of herself and her friends. She didn't accept death as a possibility.

"I'm freezing," Georgy said; he meant it literally.

Rustik walked straighter. "I'm okay except for the headache. I can walk."

Kolya and Semyon watched him as well as possible, and he did keep his balance. Then he stopped, his face even whiter than the snow. His body sagged, and he blinked his eyes sleepily. After he cocked his head as if in deep thought, he rubbed his scalp wounds and winced, looked around, and sighed.

"Igor. Wait." Rustik stopped walking.

"Move. Keep going."

Rustik raised his voice. "Listen to me. I'm dressed better than you, and I'm in better shape than anyone."

"Now's a bad time for a big ego," Lyuda said.

The wind settled except when random gusts flew at them, hammering, but the constant wail and roar eased. The snow stopped, and they realized that for a while, it had been the wind blowing the snow from the trees and upper slopes, but the actual snow storm had ended earlier. A partial slice of the moon peeked from behind the clouds and made it easier for the tourists to see their route.

"It's fact. I'm going back to the tent for supplies." Rustik held out a hand. "Hear me out.

"No," Igor said emphatically.

"Come over here, Igor, please."

Igor wondered if Rustik were about to cause a fight, but it was far worse.

Rustik spoke quietly. Close to Igor's ear. "My head is hurting, and I can't see very well anymore. I'm actually almost walking blind. My vision is messed up very badly and so is my head. I can't walk anymore. I'm done. I'm really done. I can't walk any more. That's just how it is."

"We're not letting you go back to the tent, and we're not leaving you."

"There's no choice. Think about how much energy all of you are using to keep me going. I'm exhausting you. Yuri and Georgy need help because they're in poor shape. You're struggling. Kolya, Sasha, and Semyon can't carry six people."

"I'm on my feet." Igor frowned.

"Now. If you must help carry someone, you won't be. Who'll carry Zina and Lyuda if they need help? Who'll carry Yuri and Georgy? Who'll carry you? I can't do this. Do you want to carry me or Zina?"

"Either. Both. Don't do this," Igor begged.

"I'm very aware that I'm freezing fast since I hit my head although why that is, I'm not sure. Whatever I did...cracked it good. I can't do this blind. I'm so tired and I want to rest. I need to lie down. If I could keep going, I would, and you *know* that. You do."

"I don't want to discuss this." Igor knew that if Rustik said he was too tired to keep going, he meant it. Rustik wasn't a quitter.

Rustik shrugged. "There's no choice, but it's reality. Talking to you is almost causing my head to explode. Talking hurts. Thinking hurts. I have to lie down, and once I do, I won't get up. I need to go to sleep. Brother."

"But...."

"In five minutes, I'm going to sit down. Lie down. Rest. Please don't let the others be close enough to see that. Don't let them get frantic or upset over me. Get them far enough away to prevent that. I can't handle emotional stuff from everyone. Give me that respect. Please."

Igor saw tears in Rustik's eyes, but he saw more, now. He saw that Rustik was stooped and swaying slightly, barely keeping upright. He kept his fists clenched, and Igor realized that his hands were frozen in place, and even if they were saved that second, Rustik would lose his fingers, hands, and probably parts of his arms. Toes. Feet. Maybe they'd all lose digits, but Igor knew only Rustik was a runner and he would lose the ability to be himself.

Rustik knew more than Igor about his head injury; it was probably far worse than they knew. But another fact about Rustik that Igor knew was that he never gave up; to do so was a sign that Rustik was positive he couldn't survive and was terrified of being a burden on the rest. That was how unselfish Rustik Slobodin acted.

"I can't...." Igor. Why had the head injury caused Rustik to start freezing? It wasn't fair.

"Just give me privacy."

Igor managed a slight choking noise as he swallowed hard.

"See you on the other side." Rustik tried to smile

Igor gave him a nod, looked into his eyes for a second, hoping that he expressed his feelings, and then turned, determined not to allow the others to see the pain that gripped him.

"He isn't going back alone. Igor, one of us needs to go with him," Kolya protested. "I'll go."

"No. You will help Yuri. Zina needs help with him."

Yuri and Zina spoke at once and said they didn't need help.

"Sasha, help Georgy if Lyuda can't do it alone, and Semyon, I may need your help. Keep moving." Igor continued to give orders as he walked, and the others kept up but looked back.

"I ...." Semyon caught the look in Igor's eyes and understood. "That's just not fair. Damnit. Come on. We need to pick up the pace like Igor said."

Yuri watched, listened, and then leaned over to whisper to Zina. She closed her eyes and held back wails. Lyuda took her arm in hers and sniffled.

Kolya stared straight ahead. "Igor?"

"Walk faster, and don't anyone dare look back, or else. Don't you *dare* do something that *hurtful*."

Rustik peeked back surreptitiously and was relieved that Igor kept everyone from looking back at him; had they looked back, he would have bawled and lost his nerve. He wasn't nearly as brave or unselfish; he was cold and in pain. He tripped, fell, got up, and managed a few more steps up the slope.

He had to stop falling.

It would be humorous if he made it all the way back up the slope to the tent where the blankets and warm clothing were. And the heater. Not that he could put it together with his hands locked into frozen fists, but the idea was pleasant. He would warm himself, dress better, and carry supplies back down to his friends. He would take care of them. Save them. He could do that.

No problem.

He stumbled again and fell with his arms bent and in front and sank into the snow. His bent legs wouldn't move. He couldn't lift himself up with his arms and barely raised his face to breathe. It was better to lie down.

It felt better to take a real rest.

Igor was a good man; he kept his promise to make the rest walk away without turning back to look. He understood that sympathy and pity would be worse than anything. Igor was a rarity: brilliant and good-hearted and a true friend.

Rustik wondered if the women would be okay. Yuri and Georgy were....

His head throbbed.

Igor was true in every way.

Wasn't it interesting that his hands were frozen?

How far was the tent he wondered because he needed to hurry.

The snow around him melted slightly due to the last remaining warmth in his body but would freeze as soon as he cooled.

It was a blessing that he didn't think about home or his family. He didn't pity himself. He forgot why he was in the snow, who had been with him, where he was, and what had happened. He wasn't afraid or sad. He was only sleepy.

So tired.

His watch, a Zvezda brand, stopped as it froze: the time was 8:45.

The wind gusted over Rustik; it was one of the random bursts that blew several times colder than the usual. As Rustik thought about nothing at all, his body froze. He died as peacefully as possible considering the circumstances.

In that way, he was fortunate; the rest would not fare as well.

*Author's note: Rustik had to have died first because he was the only one warm enough to die in an "icy bed", meaning his body heat melted the snow, and it froze again around him. His head injury was serious and would have accelerated organ shut-down. He was found facing the tent, and his hands had third-and-fourth-degree frostbite. His bare foot was also frostbitten. The batteries in the flashlight found on the path to the tree were dead.

Rustik S

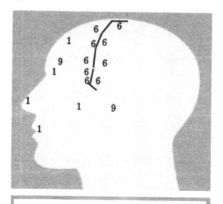

1. abrasion and bruises
2. cuts
3. 4th degree frostbite
5. burns
6. fractures
7. foam
8. post mortem:
9. other:
   bleeding

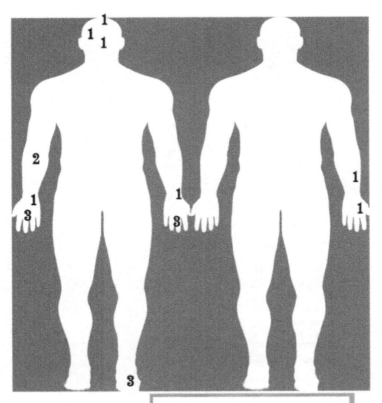

1. abrasion and bruises
2. cuts
3. 4th degree frostbite
5. burns
6. fractures
7. foam
8. post mortem:
9. other:

Rustik S

6
The Cedar: Yuri Alekseevich Krivonischenko (Georgy)

A large cedar grew at the edge of the tree line.

We made it," Igor called out. Most of them had matches either in their pockets or sewn into a pocket. Others had left their matches behind, sewn into their jackets. The wood around the tree, although it would burn well and provide a strong blaze, was damp. They were too cold and too tired to dig a fire pit, and the snow was deep; thus, it was likely that as soon as the fire became hot, the wood would melt the snow and go out.

There was no choice.

With his knife, Semyon cut way lower branches and handed them to some of the others to shake well, break, and prepare for the fire. Then, he walked around the tree and cut two dozen small trees and gathered twigs and good firewood, but there wasn't a lot on the ground. Sasha and Kolya worked beside him.

Georgy, Igor, and Yuri ignored the poor conditions of their hands and climbed the lowest limbs, scraping their inner thighs so badly that Yuri tore his pants and left skin on the bark of the tree; he barely felt the injury. Yuri climbed higher, broke branches, and tried to see the tent. It was reality, or hopeful thinking, but he was sure that he could see the tent, dark against the snow, but still standing, albeit half covered with snow and partially hidden. It had survived the winds.

Yuri called to Igor. "I can see the tent, I think. It's at least half covered by snow. The wind knocked it down in the center, but it's still where we left it."

"One of those winds could finish it off. We can't make it all the way back unless we get warm. I don't think we should try to go back."

"I can't anyway," Yuri said, as he painfully climbed down the tree, falling part of the way.

Some managed to use their body weight and fading energy to pull the branches and snap them off. Several times, Georgy fell, unable to hold on to the branches. Frostbite and 3rd and 4th degree had crept from his fingers to his hands and moved to his elbows. His toes and feet were almost fully frozen, but his body tried to survive and kept pulling heat and blood flow from the extremities to the core.

Yuri was experiencing the same.

"Sorry, I can't get more firewood," Yuri told Zina.

She shook her head. "You're too cold to climb again. You fell, so you must stop."

"I'm sorry for so much," he said sadly. He looked into her eyes.

Zina felt a lump in her throat. "Stop. No apologies right now. We can talk after we are safe again and somewhere warm."

"My hands and feet…not going to make it, Zina. You should take my sweater and socks. Get warmer."

"Please, don't."

"I need to tell you…."

Zine shook her head again. "When we are safe, tell me."

She held her hands out, closer to the fire.

The fire felt wonderful, and everyone gathered to warm before gathering more branches. It wasn't a huge fire or nearly warm enough, but it felt good, gave them much needed light, and was morally energizing.

"Can't we go back and get Rustik once we're warm?" Lyuda begged.

"I can't think about him being out there alone. Cold," Kolya agreed.

Igor stared into the flames. "You know it's too late. He was too injured, too cold, and it's what he wanted."

"Maybe he made it back to the tent, got warm, and will come back with supplies. If anyone can do it, it's Rustik." Kolya tried to smile. He lied to himself, not the others.

"Maybe. But it's a long way to go for someone who's hurt his head. Then back here…too far. And we can't depend on that. We must do what we can to survive out here. We'll depend on ourselves." Igor didn't look away from the fire.

"But he's alone," Lyuda couldn't let go yet.

Semyon spoke quietly, "The wind has settled except for the sudden bursts, and when it hits, it's cold. It's worse on the slope. Do you realize how far we've come to find firewood and shelter from the wind?"

"Yes. It's a long way, but Rustik could have made it back. Maybe. But if he didn't…." Lyuda took a breath. "He's alone."

Igor rubbed her back and tried to find comforting words, but it was impossible. "Lyuda, he can't make it back." He looked at Kolya as he spoke to include him. "He knew he was done and wanted us to get here and make a fire. He wanted us to survive when he knew he couldn't. He didn't want to burden us. He decided to spend his last bit of time alone and respectfully away from us."

Lyuda cried and leaned against Igor's shoulder.

Igor went on. "That is how unselfish he is. He's a hero and the bravest of all. And he's a good citizen. His concern was for the whole and not for himself. Remember that."

Lyuda wiped her eyes. "That's true. Don't we love him for that?"

Everyone agreed.

Sasha, Kolya, and Semyon gathered more branches, making a stack.

Igor wanted to help, but his body betrayed him. Because he was so cold, his bladder refused to void, and it caused him pain. While the result was pain, it also kept him alive as his body fought to survive and that was good. His mind betrayed him, replaying the last minutes with Rustik.

He suddenly realized that there was a strange scent in the air.

Georgy sat leaning close to the fire, his feet outstretch. He failed to realize his socks were on fire or that his leg was burned.

Igor grabbed Georgy and yanked him away from the fire; Lyuda covered Georgy's feet with snow to extinguish the burns and to soothe the pain, but he felt no pain. His feet were frozen solid. So were his legs, fingers, hands, and arms.

"Is he okay?" asked Sasha.

Zina yanked away one burned sock and tossed it away, then the second. His toes were charred. She wept as she viewed the frostbitten and burned toes. His leg was also burned. "You're so bruised." She petted his forehead gently.

"Tourist survives being on fire. That's your headline, Zina." Georgy's eyes were glassy.

His head aching furiously, looked at his hand, at the torn flesh that he couldn't feel. Georgy put his hand to his mouth and ripped away the hanging flesh with his teeth, causing Zina to cry out, but he felt nothing. While looking at her, he became numb all over. Thoughts sifted away like fine sand. He wanted to say something more, but he forgot what it was and knew it wasn't important. It wasn't sleep, but a slow loss of consciousness.

He lay back.

"Get up," Sasha ordered.

"I have to rest. I'm tired, Sasha. Don't make … get up; my feet don't want … me up. … in awful shape, aren't they? My fingers." He coughed a greyish red foam.

Georgy K

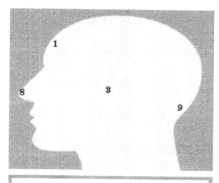

1. abrasion and bruises
2. cuts
3. 4th degree frostbite
5. burns
6. fractures
7. foam
8. post mortem:
9. other:
   blood

Sasha sat beside him and waited. "We love you, Georgy." No one else said a word.

Georgy smiled, sighed, and let go.

The others watched without knowing what to say; there was nothing they could do.

Unlike the death of Rustik, this death they saw. Not only was the loss of a dear, beloved friend like a stab in their hearts, but also, they knew that this was not the last death they would see. And next time, it could be them.

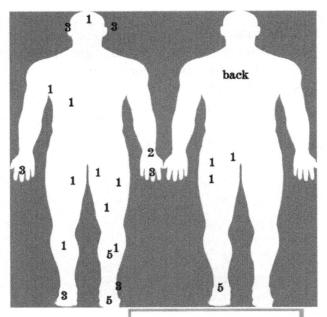

1. abrasion and bruises
2. cuts
3. 4th degree frostbite
5. burns
6. fractures
7. foam
8. post mortem:
9. other:

Georgy K

The Cedar: Yuri Nikolaevich Doroshenko

Before the others could say much or think more about the loss, Yuri rolled onto his back, setting his hair on fire. Kolya and Semyon moved fast, grabbed him, and pulled him away from the fire.

Because his blood couldn't circulate, it backed up and overfilled his heart, leaked into his lungs, and caused pulmonary edema. Blood started to fill his lungs, just like Georgy's blood had filled his lungs. "Can't breathe."

Although he spit out foamy liquid, he drowned as he froze.

Zina shook him and begged him to get warm, but he turned onto his belly and didn't move again. Zina cried out, a mournful wail.

"What just happened," Lyuda demanded. "What?"

Zina cradled Yuri's head, speaking to him as if he we alive and able to hear her. "When we get back...."

Igor put an arm around Zina.

"I don't...need help...wake them up." Lyuda refused to accept that another two of her friends were dead and had died right before her eyes. She stared.

"Lyuda," Kolya began.

She waved her hand dismissively. "Please, don't.

"They were as worried and afraid as we are, but at the end, they didn't cry in pain or say tearful goodbyes to us. They were quiet, and there was no *panic* or *pain.* They passed better than others have in this world." Igor was stoic.

"That was *Yuri* and *Georgy.* They can't be gone," Kolya was pale with sorrow.

"Is that what we can expect? I don't want to die." Lyuda was terrified. "Look at Zina and what she's going through. We can't keep dying. We *can't.*"

Semyon agreed, "Lyuda, we will find a way. We're not getting as warm as we need to be. We're too exposed and need to warm a smaller area."

"I agree," Igor said. "There should be a ravine close. In that, we could have the wood, make a good fire, stay huddled, and wait for morning."

"Then what?" Sasha asked. "We return to the tent?" He couldn't stop staring at his two dead friends, and more than anything else, he wanted to smile, sit up, and say they were just pretending.

"I doubt it's still there. We go to the *labaz*, go for help to retrieve our friends, and then go to the hospital for ourselves. We all need help. Maybe we can gather some things from the tent if we can find it, and that will help because we'll have the first aid kit, protection, the heater, and warm clothing. The winds have stopped except for the bursts of hard, cold wind. We can do this."

"Yes," Semyon said, "for the rest of the night, we make a little den and a fire and wait for the light. Everything will seem better when the sun rises."

Lyuda glanced at Yuri and Georgy, "Nothing will look better for them or for Rustik. It's too late. How will we move on now that our friends are dead?"

Zina looked at Igor. "It isn't our fault, is it?"

"No." Igor had changed their route, but that wasn't to blame. Semyon had urged them out of the tent and had cut it to get them out, and if the wind had caught the tent, then what he had done was to save their lives. There was no blame there. It was no one's fault that they had so far to go before finding firewood. They were innocent of culpability for having left the tent so fast to get to safety that they had left their warm clothing and shoes behind.

If there were anything to blame, it was nature: the wind, the noise it made, the quick freezing it caused. The snow. The storm itself and the darkness of the night it caused. The ridgeline that was slick and slippery.

Igor needed nature to help save their lives. Digging out a den in the ravine would be like a little igloo, and while not toasty, it would still be warm enough to save their lives. Hopefully. A fire, made by a den, *would* be almost toasty warm, and it *would* save their lives. Although thawing feet and hands would be extremely painful, it would be welcomed.

"How can we leave them?" Lyuda asked.

"They'd tell us to. Because that is how we survive," Kolya said, sadly. "Because we have to face reality and do whatever it takes to survive. For Rustik the strong, Yuri the brave, and Georgy the good."

Lyuda cried but reached for a lone sock and pulled it over her foot.

Semyon cut away Georgy's clothing and wrapped Lyuda's feet and helped her add Georgy's sweater over her clothing to stay warmer. He handed her other clothing, grimly nodding to her that this was the best idea. She set her jaw tightly but took the clothing.

Zina felt her heart breaking as she took some of Yuri's clothing. She held a piece to her face, inhaling his fading scent and added a pair of his socks to her feet.

Sasha and Kolya respectfully laid their friends side by side but didn't turn Yuri over; Zina didn't need to see his face again or she'd fall apart emotionally. It was painful to leave them, but the plan was solid.

After they picked up the extra cut branches, they gathered them in their arms; they couldn't carry all of them, but It was good they had a lot. Close to the place they planned to make the den, they would cut more wood for a fire before settling in to wait for the morning.

They had to leave the cedar tree.

And Georgy. And Yuri.

None were dry-eyed as they walked away.

Yuri D

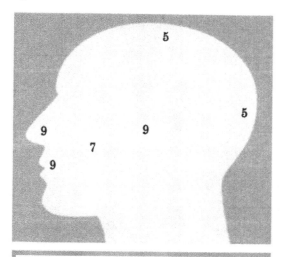

1. abrasion and bruises
2. cuts
3. 4th degree frostbite
5. burns
6. fractures
7. foam
8. post mortem:
9. other:
   blood

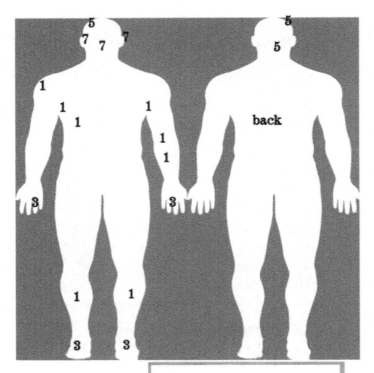

back

1. abrasion and bruises
2. cuts
3. 4th degree frostbite
5. burns
6. fractures
7. blood
7. foam
8. post mortem:
9. other:

Yuri D

8
The Ravine

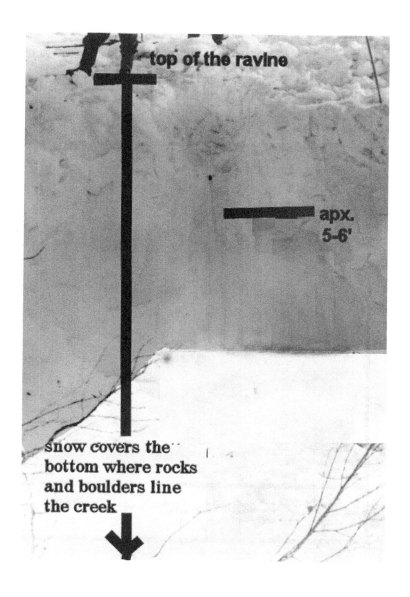

top of the ravine

apx. 5-6'

snow covers the bottom where rocks and boulders line the creek

"Here." Igor knew the right spot when he saw it. The others spoke almost in unison, all of them agreeing the ravine was perfect for a den. It was deep, covered only a little by snow, but low enough to protect everyone from the wind. There was a level spot for a fire. The water of the creek was frozen, and rocks and boulders were everywhere but easy to walk around.

Lyuda carried branches and clothing, but she had accidently dropped some of the clothing. That worried her because she wanted to use some of the clothing to wrap her feet. She planned to go back and find everything she dropped.

Dropped clothing that was discovered several months later

She and the others started to dig a den while they still had heat in their bodies and feeling in their hands. The former fire had given them enough warmth to keep them alive, and the work they did helped against the cold, but the snow that was dug away was cold and hurt their fingers.

They piled the branches into the ravine, adding the others that Semyon had cut along the way. He had thought to gather any wood they saw. They set sticks, branches, and scraps of clothing on the ground.

Once the fire was furiously burning, the small area would heat up, and the wind would stop tormenting them. They were in poor physical condition and might lose a few toes or a finger, but they would survive until morning, go to the cache, and then they would really be all right. Somehow, they would deal with the loss of three close friends and mourn them.

Except.

Lyuda was worried about her feet, and in her imagination, she kept seeing burned hair and feet; her entire body shook due to the shock of seeing her friends die so horribly.

Zina was broken-hearted and shoved her grief into the back of her mind as deeply as possible; however, while she worked as hard as two women might, her mind was far away.

Kolya missed Georgy who was a close friend and wished he could go back and save his life. And Yuri. And Rustik. He replayed the good parts of the trip in his head and forced himself to keep going. What he really wanted to do was go to see if Yuri and Georgy might be alive. That idea was unrealistic, but it plagued him.

Sasha knew that if Rustik hadn't fallen, he would be the one helping Igor the most; they had all depended on Rustik and never realized it. To honor his friend, Sasha decided to step up and to help Igor as much as possible; he feared failing.

Semyon fought himself, wondering if he had panicked needlessly and caused three deaths. What if the wind wasn't bad and the tent was standing? But at the time, he also told himself that cutting the tent and getting everyone out was the only action that made sense. "What if there was no need for this?"

Lyuda looked up. "What do you mean?"

"What if the wind didn't take the tent? What if we could have stayed there?"

"The storm was bad. The wind probably tossed the tent down the slope, and if we'd been inside it, the impact would have broken our bones. We'd have died, suffering." Lyuda frowned. "If you hadn't gotten us out, we would have died."

"Three already have," Semyon said.

"It would be nine of us dead," Sasha said. "I don't know how we'll get over the loss of three, but we're alive." He wondered how many times they had to say it aloud, much less think about what had happened so far.

"I would have ordered everyone out," Igor said. "I didn't think we had time to waste."

"We might have had time to dress. Boots and jackets." Semyon felt guilty.

Lyuda shook her head and put her hand on his back. "You did what you thought was best in order to save our lives. Thank you. It's what Igor would have done, but you did it first."

"Okay, Lyuda. I'll go get more firewood. You rest and get ready for the fire. I'll carry an extra load for you."

She smiled sadly. If only the other three were here to warm themselves. If only toes and hair didn't burn.

"Let's see if we can find a few more pieces of wood, and then we'll get the fire blazing," Igor said. He struggled with his own emotions: fear for his friends, sorrow, his guilt over his failure to save three of the group. His determination kept him moving, that and the knowledge that he had to be an effective leader, or they'd all perish. That was a fact.

"Go. Let me stay and dig a little more here. We want the den to be protective and solid," Sasha suggested. "I can dig some more."

"Are you sure?" Igor asked. Digging was particularly difficult, tiring, and cold work.

"Positive. I've got it." Sasha knew that someone had to do the hardest work and that he was positive that it should be him. He tried to ignore the fact that deep within his core, he was freezing. With all his experience and determinization, nature was in charge. He dug into the snow.

The others thanked him and left the ravine.

They picked up more branches. Semyon let the others do the cutting while he carried as much as possible, making Lyuda chide him for doing her part of the work. Lyuda, Semyon, and Kolya walked ahead of Zina and Igor as they returned to the ravine with branches, far fewer than they had hoped to find.

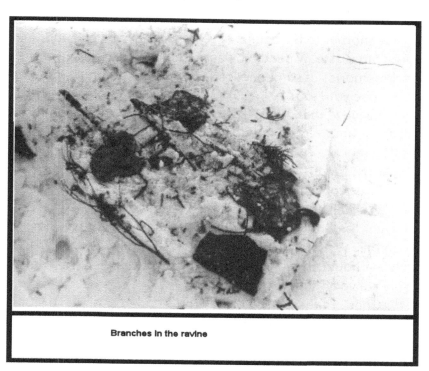

Branches in the ravine

"I'll have to go back and get the rest of the wood we left and cut more from the cedar tree," Igor said.

Zina swallowed hard. She was strong and brave, and yet some struggles were too difficult. "I can't look at Yurda again. I can't stand it." Her eyes filled with tears.

Igor patted her with his free hand. He saw how pale she was. His heart ached for her loss. "I know. I'm so sorry. Yuri was a good man."

"I already miss him so much my heart hurts."

"It will hurt badly for a long time, but then you can heal from this pain. You'll remember the good times."

Zina knew Igor hurt. It was one thing to be jealous of a living man, but another to be jealous of someone he had liked and admired but was now dead. It was awful to have to resent the perfect memories of someone lost. She had to say what was in her heart. "I love you, too."

"I believe that. It's awful to care so much about two people, at the same time," Igor sympathized. He couldn't find it within himself to feel anger toward a friend recently dead. "I love you as well. I've lost friends tonight who I love with all my heart."

It was unlike him to be emotional.

"We'll all be okay now, right? The rest of us?"

Igor told her what she needed to hear. "Of course. We'll get through this. We'll tell their families that they died heroically and bravely, without complaining and without much pain. We'll never say how we've all suffered."

"Good. That's what...." Zina words ended as she and Igor approached the den from the shallower side. Something distracted her. The others were approaching the ravine in the wrong way, it seemed. Maybe they were going to follow the ridgeline down to the creek.

She was wrong.

Lyuda, Semyon, and Kolya walked to the edge of the ravine to hand the branches to Sasha and then went to look for more firewood. Lyuda refused to stop helping, despite Semyon's protests.

A small force of wind whipped down the slope, causing the trio to stumble. It was forceful. Beneath their feet, the stones and soil shifted, raining into the ravine, and the snow behind them slid. It wasn't an avalanche, but it was a sliding mass that, with the wind, caught them when they were unbalanced on the scrum of rocks.

Lyuda screamed and tried to jump free as her frozen feet failed to find a solid area to stop her slide. Semyon turned slightly, hoping to regain his footing, and his knife and the branches went flying. Time stood still as he kept turning, trying to see about Lyuda who didn't stop screaming.

Pushed by the wind, Kolya slid full force, never being able to catch himself and was only aware of feeling open air and a lack of gravity or solid ground underneath him. His feet had slid back, and he fell head first through a nothingness.

Lyuda landed on a rough, large boulder without catching herself with her arms. Her breath whooshed out as her rib cage took the full force of her attempted jump and then her fatal fall. She couldn't scream with the pain but could only slide down on her knees, still leaning on the boulder. She thought about getting up, but the slightest movement was torture, so she hugged the boulder and wept. Her chest felt as if it were crushed.

She moaned as Zina ran to her and touched her back, asking her if she could move.

"Lyuda, please let me help you lie down," Zina begged. She didn't know what injuries her friend had. "Can I help you?"

When Zina lifted Lyuda's head back to check her, Lyuda moaned, although within her head, it was a wail of pain. "No." Saying one word took massive effort and was unclear.

Zina didn't understand the response and realized the injuries were massive. What she saw made her feel colder.

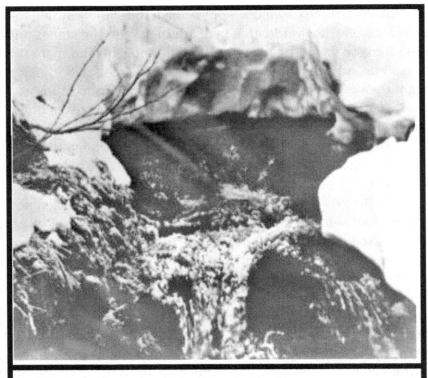

The boulder. The water was frozen when she fell.

When Lyuda landed on the rock, she bit her own tongue off. Blood ran from Lyuda's mouth as her face settled back against the stones; fortunately, she went into shock that took away the terrible agony. Lyuda never realized that she had bitten away her own tongue. Each breath was agony, but her mind had shut down.

Blood ran down her throat. Four ribs on her right side were broken. On her left, six ribs were fractured, and the top one caused the right atrium of her heart to bleed.

Sasha was caught across the side of his neck by Semyon's leg as Semyon fell. Sasha fell backward, violently striking the back of his head on a rock. For several minutes, he was stunned, dizzy, in pain, and frightened. He was semi-conscious.

Semyon hit a large boulder when he fell. The fall was so bad that he almost crushed the right side of his ribcage. The bones were broken so badly that it took a massive effort for him to roll onto his back. He moaned, unable to move at all after shifting to his back. When he bounced after hitting the boulder and landing on his back, the force was still so great that he hit his head hard enough to cut it deeply, almost to the skull.

Igor tried to do something as he knelt by Semyon but felt useless. His hands were freezing, literally, and he was sure that he wouldn't be able to make a fire by himself. Semyon was hurt badly, and Igor was unsure how to help. He had no medical supplies, couldn't make a fire, and was nearly speechless with sorrow and fear. What a failure he was in his mind. "Semyon?"

Rocks and boulders on the ravine's bottom.

"I'm in awful trouble," Semyon whispered quietly. It was painful to speak, but he did his best. It was difficult to focus on anything but the pain.

"What can I do?"

Semyon knew he was badly injured and would not be able to get up again. He knew the fall had cost him his life. "Are Lyuda and Kolya all right?"

Igor lied, "They'll be fine. I'm worried about you. Can you sit up?"

"No. I'm sure I've broken all my ribs...my head. I won't be getting up." Semyon was becoming more tired as he spoke. And so cold. He knew he was finished, wanted to sleep and escape the pain, but he was also very afraid and sad.

"I want to help," Igor said. How he could help, he didn't know, and that frustrated him.

"You're a fine leader. A friend. Just sit beside...for a while? Talk... me a little?"

Igor said he would. He glanced at Zina, and she gave him a shake of her head. He knew that Lyuda was injured very badly and that Zina meant that there was no hope. Igor gave Zina a shake of his head, too. He knew that Semyon was indeed in trouble, and it was serious.

Of all the nine tourists, Semyon had been the best dressed. He and Kolya. Semyon had gotten them free of the tent when he was terrified of the storm. Instead of running away to save himself, which would have been better in the long run, Semyon bravely thought first of his friends. Of everyone, he had been in the best shape as far as lack of injuries and warmer clothing; he could have survived with a fire built next to the den. Igor felt sick to his soul.

"Sasha. How are you?" Igor called.

"Just a little headache. I'm doing fine. I can get up now. How's Semyon?" Sasha stumbled to his feet.

Igor shook his head again emphatically. "I'm just sitting here with him a while, as he asked. He's resting."

Sasha nodded that he understood. He was numb all over. "Zina? Lyuda?" Sasha asked.

"Lyuda isn't feeling well. She's resting here where she fell. She doesn't feel like moving." Zina didn't want to cause Lyuda more fear if she said something more, but behind Lyuda's back, she was able to give Sasha a shake of her head, the same as Igor had.

"Can Kolya get up? How is he? Kolya, I need your help," Igor called.

Sasha knelt by Kolya. He shook his friend. Nothing. "Kolya? Wake up."

Kolya didn't move. His face remained passive.

Sasha felt for a pulse and found no beat in Kolya's cold wrist or neck. He raised his head and roared. "No. No. No. No. No."

"Oh, God," Igor moaned.

Zina closed her eyes and grit her teeth.

"Not Kolya. Not him." Sasha wept for him, but also for Georgy, Rustik, Yuri, Lyuda, and Semyon. Mostly he wept for the sweetest member of the group. Their heart.

Nicolay Thibeaux Brignolle (Kolya)

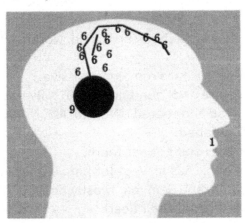

* Kolya T-B

1. abrasion and bruises
2. cuts
3. 4th degree frostbite
5. burns
6. fractures
7. foam
8. post mortem:
9. other:
   bleeding

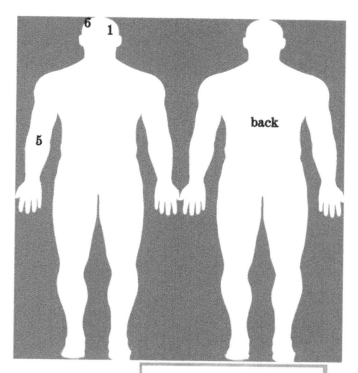

1. abrasion and bruises
2. cuts
3. 4th degree frostbite
5. burns
6. fractures
7. foam
8. post mortem:
9. other:

Kolya T-B

Lyudmila Alexandrovna Dubinina (Lyuda)

Lyuda D

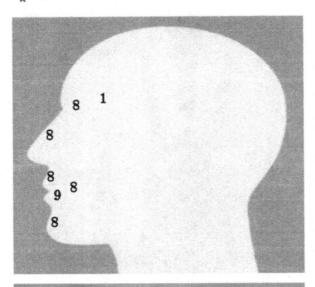

1. abrasion and bruises
2. cuts
3. 4th degree frostbite
5. burns
6. fractures
7. foam
8. post mortem:
9. other:
   part of tongue missing

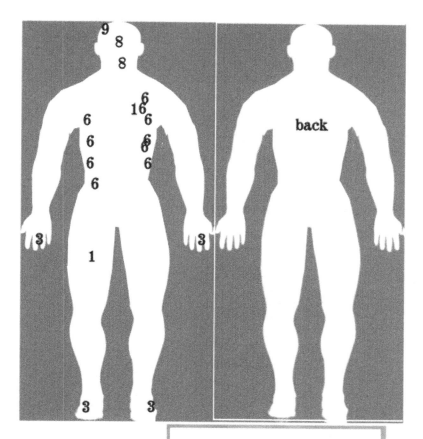

1. abrasion and bruises
2. cuts
3. 4th degree frostbite
5. burns
6. fractures
7. foam
8. post mortem:
9. other:

Lyuda D

She's gone. That's merciful," Zina declared a minutes later. She wanted to scream for Lyuda, but she couldn't let go of her rage; it was all that was keeping her going.

"I'm afraid," Semyon whispered.

"Don't be. Be at peace. I'm with you," Igor said.

"The war...." Semyon stopped speaking and let out a long, rattling breath. His heart had bled, and he died of massive injuries and hypothermia.

Semyon Aleksandrovich Zolotaryov

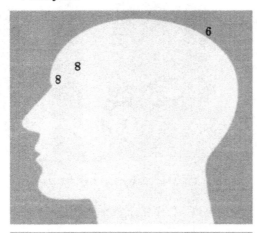

* Semyon Z

1. abrasion and bruises
2. cuts
3. 4th degree frostbite
5. burns
6. fractures
7. foam
8. post mortem:
9. other:

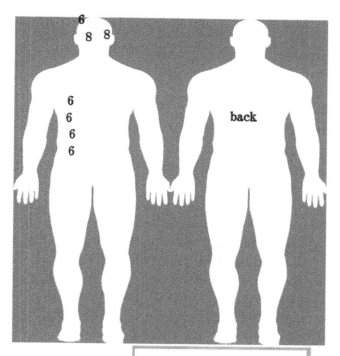

back

1. abrasion and bruises
2. cuts
3. 4th degree frostbite
5. burns
6. fractures
7. foam
8. post mortem:
9. other:

Seymon Z

missing eyes #8

Zina walked over to Igor. She stared at the ground.

"Look at your hands," Igor said. "Wrap them. You have to save them."

"I'm in fine shape. I can't imagine what our feet look like."

"I can live without a few toes," Igor joked.

Zina didn't laugh.

Sasha stared straight ahead.

"Sasha, let me see your head," Zina ordered.

She checked the wound, and although it was painful and looked bad, it wasn't a serious head wound. Normally, he'd receive medical attention and recover, but with the cold, it complicated the hypothermia. She knew they needed to make a fire, but she kept looking from Lyuda to Kolya to Semyon and back to Sasha.

One of his woolen socks was burned, and even though he also wore cotton socks, his feet were fully frozen. He wasn't sure when he burned his sock and wondered if he had burned his foot at the fire by the cedar tree. Maybe. If they were rescued right that second, he'd lose his feet, not just toes. Likely he'd lose his entire lower legs. His hands were numb. He supposed he'd lose them as well. Maybe his upper arms. He would probably lose parts of his face: sections of his cheeks, his nose.

He didn't want to live that way.

The most reserved member of the team cried openly. Seeing Lyuda and Kolya broke his spirit. He had felt strongly for Lyuda and had never told her or shown it. It was now too late. It was too late for so much.

And moreover, they had failed. They had all failed to summit Mount Otorten. *He* had failed.

"I'm so tired."

"I know, but I'm about to build a fire, okay?" Igor said.

"I'm not that cold now." Sasha leaned over next to Semyon and lay down. It felt good to rest.

"Get up. Get up right now, Sasha."

Sasha didn't respond. He closed his eyes.

Aleksander Sergeevich Kolevatov (Sasha)

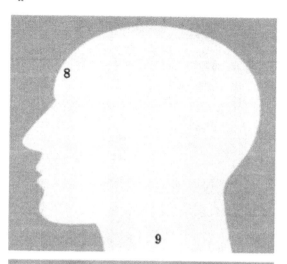

Sasha K

1. abrasion and bruises
2. cuts
3. 4th degree frostbite
5. burns
6. fractures
7. foam
8. post mortem:
9. other:
   injury

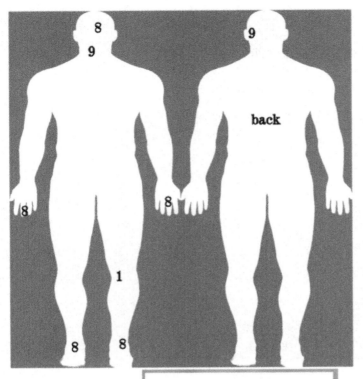

1. abrasion and bruises
2. cuts
3. 4th degree frostbite
5. burns
6. fractures
7. foam
8. post mortem:
9. other:
   injury

Sasha K

The Slope

Zina didn't try to force Sasha to get up. She understood he was too tired physically and mentally to keep going. She said, "Igor, we have to get the fire going and get into the den."

Igor looked at Sasha. His eyes were glazed, and his mind was far away. Like Sasha, he felt guilty and ashamed that they failed to summit the mountain, but he also felt guilt for the deaths of his friends. He had deviated the course. He set the tent up far from firewood. He panicked when the wind blew so hard and followed Semyon blindly. He didn't get everyone dressed first. He left the cedar tree and led the others to the ravine. He left Rustik to die alone. He told himself that every death was his fault.

Zina would die, too. He had inadvertently killed someone he loved the most.

Like a sleep walker and as broken in his mind as Sasha had been, Igor looked up. His face was blank, his eyes far away as in his mind, and he saw Mount Otorten just ahead. Igor was about to summit, and his friends behind him would celebrate alongside of him. The mountain was so close. He had to finish.

He walked out of the ravine even though Zina called to him.

Like a captain who goes down with his ship, Igor had to go down with his failed expedition.

His thoughts were not valid; he wasn't to blame for everything that happened, not even the deaths. His various injuries, hypothermia, and pulmonary edema were causing irrational thoughts. Heart break and exhaustion ruled his thoughts. Mentally, he was in shock and was little more than a dead man walking, albeit a good man and good leader.

Zina stood in the ravine for a very long time, unsure what to do. She could build a fire. She could survive. She needed to tell their story, so everyone understood how bravely each person fought. How each died with those who loved them.

But she didn't want to be alone. Alone was worse than anything. Who would be with her if she died? And who would be with Igor? She loved him too much to allow him to be alone; he wasn't like Rustik. Igor needed her.

She said a sad farewell to her friends in the ravine, gathered her inner strength, and walked out of the ravine in the same direction as Igor. Toward the tent, up the slope.

She trudged in the snow.

Igor was lying face down in the snow when she found him. His fists were raised as if he were fighting the cold like a foe. She was too late. She didn't know that when he had died, his blood pooled, and then it had frozen immediately. He had died rapidly and without suffering.

She rolled him over and gave him a kiss. "Rest easy, darling." She continued.

Igor Alekseevich Dyatlov

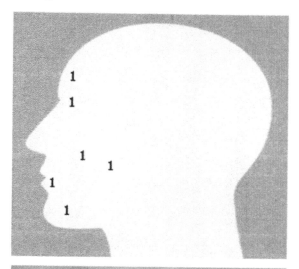

* Igor D

1. abrasion and bruises
2. cuts
3. 4th degree frostbite
5. burns
6. fractures
7. foam
8. post mortem:
9. other:

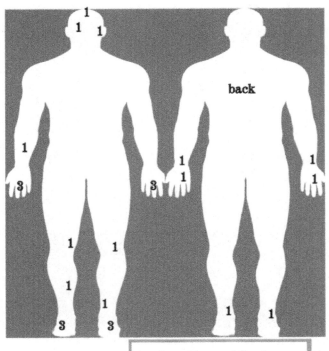

1. abrasion and bruises
2. cuts
3. 4th degree frostbite
5. burns
6. fractures
7. foam
8. post mortem:
9. other:

Igor D

Zina walked away. She had to get to the tent. The tent was a good place, and she could get warm. It made sense to her. The tent couldn't be far. If it still stood. Maybe. Probably not.

She was less than a third of the way when she fell.

It was okay. She needed to rest.

The oddest thought entered her mind. She wished she weren't a virgin and had made love with Yurda or Igor. Yes. She loved children and could have had two. No. Four. Two boys and two girls. Beautiful babies with her mouth and nose and their father's eyes. Tall, healthy, perfect children. She imagined how lovely it would be as a mother. She'd be a good wife to her real love. She laughed a little.

Four children, all happy and smart. As brave as their daddy.

She thought of how her wedding would look and wondered how wonderful it would have been. Her dress... It didn't enter her mind that the two men who were candidates for a husband were dead.

As hypothermia claimed her, and she let go, she managed to curl up, dreaming of a magical life.

Zanaida Alekseevna Kolmogorova (Zina)

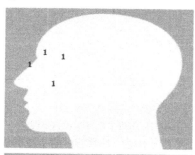

1. abrasion and bruises
2. cuts
3. 4th degree frostbite
5. burns
6. fractures
7. foam
8. post mortem:
9. other:

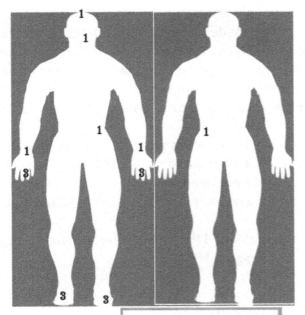

1. abrasion and bruises
2. cuts
3. 4th degree frostbite
5. burns
6. fractures
7. foam
8. post mortem:
9. other:

Zina K

*Author's note: The order of deaths has been fiercely debated. My theory is probably one of the most different. I believe it was Rustik who died first.

Yuri and Georgy died next. Whether the others went to build the den and left them a while or stayed by the fire or even split up (Yuri and Georgy at the tree) (Lyuda, Semyon, Sasha, Koyla at the ravine) (Zina, Igor trying for the tent) (Rustik?) is also debated. It seems illogical that anyone left the warm fire at first. We know that there were branches cut for the fire and ready to be burned at the cedar tree and the ravine.

Yuri and Georgy died of hypothermia. Both knew when they left the tent that they were doomed but went anyway. They died next because of the clothing that was taken by the others and because the bodies were moved post mortem.

Lyuda, Semyon, and Kolya suffered terrible injuries, and that tragedy must have happened to them at about the same time. A serious fall from the top of the ravine to the rocks below is logical and fits the evidence. The forensics match. The cause of the fall must have been the strong wind and the edge of the ravine was crumbling.

Sasha died of hypothermia but did have the neck and head injury. My theory explains this. Although I can't prove that he died seventh, it fits the timeline and with the group dynamics. Igor and Zina wouldn't have left him alone to die.

Igor was in poor condition. Only his leadership skills, experience, and sheer stubbornness got him as far allowed him to live as long as he did.

Zina and Igor could have died on the slope on the way to the cedar. I concede that possibility that neither made it very far. However, because of the body positions when they were found, they either made it to the fire and maybe to the ravine and turned back to try for the tent, OR they died on the slope when they tried to go back.

Since I've gotten to understand these people, I don't feel that either one would have turned back alone to try for the tent. They were both invested in the whole of the group. No one would have allowed Zina to go back alone. Igor wouldn't have left his friends to return alone, thus I feel I have the death timeline correct.

Enhanced photo to show the depth of the ravine. Those are shovels and a ten-foot pole used to probe the snow when searching for bodies. The top of the ravine does not show, and this is the higher part. Semyon, Sasha, and Kolya were found lower in the creek, and Lyuda was found against a boulder that was much lower. The ravine was very deep.

Part III
Search and Recovery

Weeks passed before the first five bodies were located a few miles from the summit of Otorten Mountain located in the Ural Mountains of Siberia. Months passed before the final four were found. Because originally, searchers planned a search and rescue, then a search and recovery, a lot of evidence wasn't photographed or preserved. No one expected for a great mystery to unfold.

Witness testified: Answering the questions at hand. *"On February 21, 1959 I learned from the Secretary of the Ivdel CC CPSUCcomrade Prodanov that a group of nine tourists did not return to the Polytechnic Institute from a trip to Sverdlovsk. I took measures to clarify where the students were moving and sent for support of the members of the CPSU Central Committee citizen Dryahlyh on a helicopter to search for the students. He had to look for traces of the tourists and the tourists themselves and determine the direction of their movement. Comrade Dryahlyh knows well the area of the Ivdel district. For two days he flew by helicopter north of Ivdel. He explained to me that a group of tourists passed through the village of Vizhay, Bakhtiyarov yurts, which are located several dozen kilometers from Vizhay. He could not find any traces of the tourists. Soon the search party from the Polytechnic Institute arrived from Sverdlovsk. I set before them the task of immediately organizing search units and starting the search for students."*

Because it was 1959, forensics was less than in its infancy. Autopsy reports are incomplete, remarks are unspecific, and photographs are lacking. The pathologist did believe that six deaths were at least partially due to hypothermia while three were the result of a tremendous force that broke bones and caused head injuries. All the bodies showed trauma. The last four that were found showed advanced decomposition.

But the mystery became much larger.

Why were nearly all of them found underdressed for the -25 F degree (and windchill) weather. Not only did they leave coats, hats, and mittens at the tent, they left socks and shoes behind. Why was the tent cut? And more than anything else, there was the question of why the partially dressed nine left the tent at all to travel over a mile. At night. In the cold. Without light.

Why did they leave together but were found separated?

The location of the ravine remains a debated factor.

The Search (tent): In late February, after complaints that the tourists were far overdue, a search party was formed and included airplanes and some students. Georgiy Semymonovich Ortyukov was placed in charge. Within a day, prison guards joined the search.

On February 25, ski tracks were found by Boris Slovobtzov, UPI student, and his group, who had been dropped off by helicopter on Mount Otorten. Not finding any signs of the group such as a tent, flags, belongings, or people, the group moved their search to a lower area which caused the beginning of the true search for missing tourists.

The tent was located on February 26 on slope Kholat Syakhl.

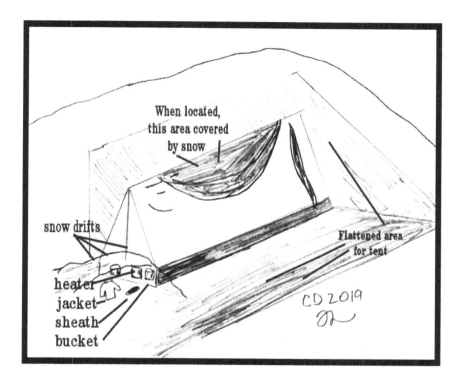

The tent was partially fallen, and the center was covered in snow, yet clearly it hadn't been ruined by an avalanche because skies and poles were standing upright. In the twenty-six days since the tragedy, snow drifts and winds had done damage. For some reason, the searchers used ice axes and shovels to open the tent, cutting it.

Whatever the reason, they acted impulsively, which is understandable.

Inside the tent were supplies, clothing, food, wood for the heater, the heater (not vented or workable), and journals. The rescue team saw ski boots and felt boots as well as jackets, but none of the missing tourists. Each of those at the site wondered why everything was left behind and knew that their search and rescue mission was probably becoming a search and recovery effort.

Contents removed from tent:

1.Camera "Sharp" with a tripod and a broken filter. Camera № 488797. Filmed 34 frames.
2. Camera "Sharp" № 486963. Filmed 27 frames. On the case deep scratches. Strap is torn.
3. Camera "Sharp" № 55149239. Filmed 27 frames.
4. Hand compass
5. Railway and bus tickets
6. Field bag
7. Flashlight electric
8. Two tins with wires
9. Diary of Slobodin
10. Money in the amount of nine hundred seventy-five rubles
11. Diary of Kolmogorova
12. Protocol Routing Commission
13. Letter with Dyatlov's name
14. The route book
15. Sealed bank. In it 10 films, a roll of film, and money in the amount of seven hundred rubles
16. Trip assignment in Dyatlov's name.
17. Maps, tracing paper, and photocopies, 9 pieces
18. Expedition plan
19. A cover letter from the Trade Union of the Institute
20. Passport in Dyatlov's name
21. Money and a letter from the Department of Trade of the city executive committee.

Rustik's diary contained only:

Notebook
To the restless mechanical Rustik
  for his diary

Northern Ural
1959
Sverdlovsk – Vizhay –

Airplane ticket
Ivdel - Saranpaul 250 rubli
(cargo free)

Mansi words

~~Oyk~~ If in the name of the mountain there is nyer - means the top (stone) is bare
oyka - ~~muzhik~~, man, husband ushnik - Mansi hunting house for warming Tol - ya - talaya creek

sos - stream, together ruma – friend nache (nashte) – hello hum – muzhik
yani – big mais – small ekva – woman ekvat – alone ayrish - girlnyan – bread
emas – good saka emas - very good
mol – bad sol – true solval – salt at – negation at-sol - not true pud – pot
vat – water vit – wind hul – fish neul – meat sali – deer vazhenka - deer doe
sohta - alpha male sun – sled sushep - look
pyrya - scram (to the dog) pisal – gun sayrep – axe mayen - give me atim - don't have oli - have
teynkvem – eat aim- drink huem – sleep eri – must ergen – sing alna – money selkoviy - ruble
akvat – 1 kita – 2 hurum – 3 nila – 4 at – 5 hot – 6 sat – 7 vovel – 8 nevel – 9 pul - 10
tinalil – eat yuvtilum – sell sup gacha – pants yelsup – dress neks – sable kutya – dog
suevat – pinery suy – pine vor – forest vorhum - bear forest man ul – fish kat – hands layal - legs
pum – head pumk – teeth palin – ears ayemun - disease, large saam - eyes nyel - nose
ayserm – cold polem – freezing kur – stove paltem – heat chuval - open chimney in the corner

Othello
Othello, the Moor of Venetia
Often visited a small house.
Shakespeare learned about it.
and wrote (scribble) a vaudeville
The girl was called Desdemona
Blushing and slender.
On the general's shoulder straps,
Oh, she was tempted.
~~Девчон~~ Her daddy - Doge of Venetia
Daddy he loved to eat,
Daddy he loved Dutch cheese,
Moscow *vodka to drink.

Outside the tent was a flashlight still in working order, a jacket near the entrance, and a knife's sheath. Three Finnish knives in their sheaths remained in the tent, so the fourth sheath belonged to someone else.

There were footprints, either those of the searchers or the tourists. A little way down the slope, older footprints led away from the tent. The searchers were shocked to see that some of the tracks were clearly made by bare feet, and there was a small handprint left by one of the women. The prints, seven or eight sets for sure, continued for a long way.

"When we finished taking inventory of the tent's contents, we moved it to the helicopter pad, about 600-700 meters away." Radiogram: *"We managed to identify footprints of eight or nine people starting from the tent and going about 1 km down the slope, and then they were lost. One person was in boots, the others were only in socks and barefoot."*

"First, we lost, and then we found, the tracks again. They appeared again in the birch-tree undergrowth, and then they went down along the ravine which led to
the Lozva River."

" When they crossed a stony ridge where the tracks disappeared, but further down they appeared again, and then they were lost. The prints were very distinct. In some of the prints one could see whether the person was barefoot or in socks because you could see the toes."

Natives of the area, Mansi, joined the rescue/recovery efforts. Tents and supplies were delivered to the site for the searchers.

The Search (cedar tree): On February 27, the searchers discovered the first two tourists 1500 meters, or 1640 yards, from the tent at the boundary of the tree line.

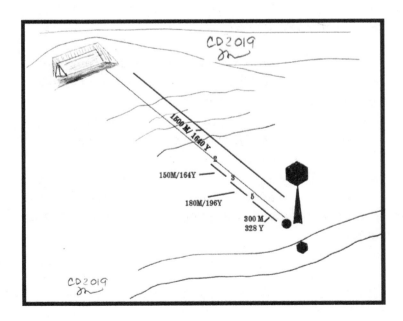

The searchers saw something dark on a flat area; it was the remains of a fire. For a second, hope bloomed, but then they saw a body.

Yuri lay on his stomach and was covered by snow, dressed in only his checked shirt, an undershirt, shorts, torn pants, and burned socks. Georgy was next to him, face up, also covered in snow. He wore only a shirt, undershirt, torn pants, and one burned sock. It was heartbreaking to find the men.

The searchers couldn't imagine what had happened. Besides the fact that the group left the tent for some mysterious reason, why had they not returned to the tent? The fire looked good and would have burned several hours, and there were more branches around the tree as well as some firewood piled up. The men froze anyway and didn't keep the fire going; it was confusing. After removing the snow, the searches didn't see any more bodies and found a strange clue: Clothing had been cut off the bodies.

It meant that the others had to be alive after the deaths of Yuri and Georgy and used the clothing to try to survive.

" Krivonischenko's right leg has no footwear. On his left foot there is a brown sock, torn. Another sock like this was discovered half burnt next to the fire. On the backs of his hands the skin is torn. Between the fingers there is blood. The index finger is also torn. The skin of the left shin is torn and covered in blood."

"Doroshenko has woolen socks on his feet, and over these socks another lighter sock. His ear, lips and nose are covered in blood, and on his left hand, the middle finger is bloody."

" Next to the bodies was a fire. Nearby were more than ten small fir tree branches, cut with a Finnish knife. The lower dry branches, of about 5 cm diameter, had been cut from the cedar. Some of these were lying next to the fire. The snow around was trampled."

" It's possible to conclude that other people had since been by the fire. We found various garments next to it rather than on the bodies, but we didn't find any other bodies. The trees near the fire had been cut with knives, but we found no knives with the bodies."

" For about 20 m around the cedar, there was evidence of young fir-trees being cut with a knife. We saw around 20 such cut stumps. But we didn't see any of the cut branches left, except for one. It isn't possible to imagine they were used to maintain the fire. First, they are not good for firewood. Second, around them were quite a lot of dry twigs and materials."

" All the low branches of the cedar within arm's reach were broken completely. One was cut 4 or 5 m high. They were thick. These types of branches are extremely difficult to brea, even if, for instance, you hang on them with the whole weight of your body."

" The lower dry branches of the cedar were broken up to 2 m high. Somebody climbed the tree because the branches 4 or 5 m high were also broken."

The search (slope): The searchers moved their efforts to the area between the tree and the slope, eyeing the tent area as they worked. They found a flashlight in the on position.

Next, they made another gruesome discovery three hundred meters (328 yards) from the tree and toward the tent.

Igor. He was face-up, but he didn't look natural because his hands were raised. One arm showed above the snow, pushed upward by a birch branch, but both arms were bent horizontally. His knees were bent, and his head was tilted back. Hands and legs don't remain raised after death; therefore, he was at least turned after death.

The searchers felt that he had been moved after death, like the men next to the cedar tree.

His Zvezda watch had stopped at 5:31.

Zina.

She was lying on her right side, dressed well except she was missing a jacket and boots, and had made it twice as far as Igor. Georgy's clothing had kept her alive longer than Igor.

Her arms were bent at her elbows, her right knee was bent more than the left, and she was curled inward. Her fingers showed 4th degree frostbite. (frostbite occurs in stages. Skin becomes cold and red, then numb, and then hard and pale. 4th degree frostbite means that the skin, muscles, and bones are frozen and dead; the area becomes black.)

Conditions were so poor that some could hardly walk.
Searcher use metal detectors and fail. They turn to ten-foot poles.

As searchers grew tired and weather conditions became worse, the search stalled.

March 2, the cache of supplies

. Condensed milk 2.5 kg

. Meat canned banks 4 kg

. Sugar - 8 kg

. Butter - 4 kg

. Cooked sausage - 4 kg

. Salt - 1.5 kg

. Kissel-compote - 3 kg

. Oatmeal and buckwheat 7.5 kg

. Cocoa 200 g

0. Coffee - 200 g

1. Tea - 200 gr

2. Loin - 3 kg

3. Milk powder - 1 kg

4. Sugar - 3 kg

5. Crackers - 7 kg and Noodles - 5 kg

6. Also found: mandolin, a pair of shoes 41 size, and worn socks inside, pair of insulated boots (Dyatlov's), mounting set, 2 batteries mounted with the bulb for lighting, extra skis, and firewood.

March 4, autopsies were done for Yuri, Georgy, Igor, and Zina.

On March 5, Rustik was located. The searchers knew that he was warm when he died because of the melted-then-frozen snow around him, the death bed or corpse-bed. His watched had stopped at 8:45.

His head was tilted back, one arm was bent, one was straight, and both hands were in fists. His face was relaxed.

His autopsy was March 8.

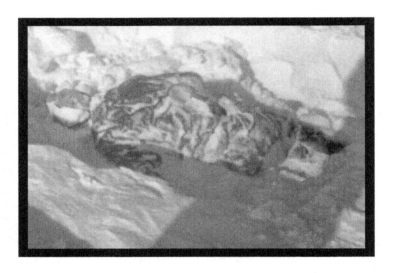

Over March 9 and 10, the five were buried.

On March 17 the lead investigator was fired, and Lev Ivanov replaced him.

Nothing happened throughout April.

The Search: (ravine): On May 5, over three months after their deaths, Lyuda, Semyon, Sasha, and Kolya were finally located by a cadaver dog as the snow began to melt. A trail of broken and cut branches made a trail to a deep ravine. Items of clothing were found along the trail to include: a leg of a pair of black ski pants, a thick brown wool sweater a white wool sweater, and a pair of brown pants.

"The bodies were found few meters away from the clothes found of Krivonischenko and Doroshenko - pants, sweater. All clothes had been cut when they were taken from the bodies of Doroshenko and Krivonischenko. Bodies of Thibault-Brignoles and Zolotaryov were better dressed, Dubinina's fur jacket and hat were found on Zolotaryov, her leg was wrapped in woolen trousers that belong to Krivonischenko. Krivonischenko's knife was found close to the bodies, it was used to cut off branches of young fir trees."

Lyuda was located first and was positioned against a boulder with her head turned slightly, and her weight on her knees. Her eyes and tongue and much of her face were missing, but she was amid decomposition and lying in running water.

The other three bodies were located close together and above where Lyuda was located. Semyon's eyes were missing, likely due to birds or water damage.

"The bodies are decaying, and we have photographed them. They need to be taken out of the stream immediately because they are decaying fast and will soon be lost in the stream, which is very fast."

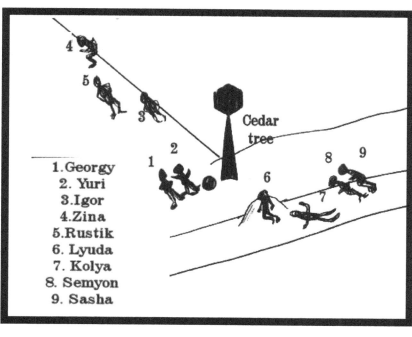

1. Georgy
2. Yuri
3. Igor
4. Zina
5. Rustik
6. Lyuda
7. Kolya
8. Semyon
9. Sasha

Cedar
tree

Part IV

Defence of My Theory

We will probably never know, or agree, about what happened to the Dyatlov Nine.

The searchers hoped for a rescue; by the time they realized it was a recovery, evidence was lost. After that, they thought it had to be a terrible natural disaster and went into recovery mode. No one thought it would be classified as a crime scene, then "solved" without satisfying anyone involved. The decisions were poor but were based on inexperience, shock, sorrow, and deteriorations in the weather. It just happened, and no one knew how to secure the scenes or how to collect evidence or that they needed to do either.

"Securing and preserving as much evidence as possible is key. With a crime scene that was exposed to the elements, they have already lost so much evidence it becomes even more important to preserve what they can find. Video and photograph documentation of every detail is paramount." (DA Roberts)

Psychology: Brad Hammock recently summited Mount Charleston, Griffith Peek, and Mummy Mountain which are all over 10Ks. He has years of experience with the sport and explained the psychology behind what he does. It helped me gain deeper insight into exactly what the tourists felt during their trip, how goal-oriented they were, and why they loved the sport.

"It's a way to perceive life. The experience is the struggle and the fulfilment once you reach the summit. When the wind blows through the trees it feels like the mountains are speaking to you."

What he said was that both the struggle and the fulfillment ital. This explains why the group wasn't satisfied with an easy ᴧcursion; they were long passed that, and it would offer no true experience worth having. The summit brings accomplishment, but not if there is no difficulty. Although the university later took heavy hits and some instructors were fired for allowing the trip in those conditions, the Dyatlov Nine craved the challenge.

Hypoxia: My theory adds this without me explicitly saying that was part of what happened to cause the tourists to rush from the tent. It is very possible at 10K.

Love: I don't know what Zina felt for either Yuri or Igor, but I can surmise. It's a fact that she dated Yuri, they met each other's families, and for some reason he broke off the relationship. Her diary is not written in a prolific way, but she did manage to make note of their talking and that he was a flirt. She didn't seem to mind. And since he did flirt, he still cared at some level.

Igor's photograph of Zina that he kept in his journal shows that he cared about her as more than a friend. They spent a lot of time together on campus, but there is no indication in her diary that she cared as much for him as she did Yuri.

It's possible that she loved them both or loved the concept of being in love. Regardless, the loss of both men, as well as the loss of six other close friends and one new friend was devastating.

Relationships: All evidence shows that eight of the tourists were very good friends. There is nothing to indicate that anyone disliked Semyon once they got to know him. I can allow for arguments and even fist fights, but it is illogical to think that anyone of the group turned on the others. There is no evidence of that. While a set of footprints veers away, they return, and there was no sign of an altercation.

Tent: Some will argue to the death that the cuts on the tent were made from the inside and that they indicate blind panic. I don't agree.

The tent is no longer in evidence because supposedly it became molded and was thrown away.

The few pictures are far too few to show enough evidence. There are no photographs with a ruler or meter stick/yardstick to show the measurements of the cuts. There are no measurements to show the locations of the cuts. There are no pictures from the inside of the tent. There were no tests to recreate the damage or to identify the instrument.

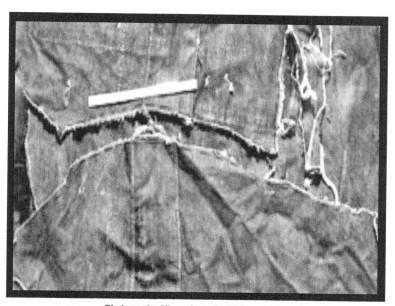

Photograph of the cuts on the tent.

DA Roberts, a current sheriff's deputy and former law enforcement supervisor, explained:

I would look at the fibers to indicate direction of cuts and the type of instrument used to make the cuts. I would also look for signs of blood or other fluids to indicate the presence of the victims and/or possible attackers.

Note: First he mentioned the fibers. There was some investigation into how fibers are cut as opposed to torn, but fibers can and have helped investigations understand the direction and may even give clues to the handedness of the cutter.

Next, he brings up the type of instrument. A razor, a Finnish knife, an axe, a penknife, an ice axe, and a shovel make different cuts. How can anyone be sure what was used? That is basic. It's logical and appears in some evidence that the shovel and maybe an axe or an ice axe made some of the cuts when the tent was uncovered. What made the other cuts? Using a pen knife certainly would be unusual when three Finnish knives were found inside and in sheaths. It would be very slow to cut through the canvas with a pen knife.

A fourth Finnish knife that was used from the outside makes the most sense. Semyon, as a former military man, would most likely have carried a weapon.

Roberts then mentions signs of blood and other fluids.

Although not related to the tent, neither woman was raped, and the evidence is not indicative of any sexual activity. That takes one fluid out of the possibilities.

At least one searcher said there was urine outside the tent or close by. Whether or not the snow would have covered that is unknown because the situation was not recreated to test that possibility. Of course, there had to be urine in areas around the tent, but why there would be only one place noted is suspect. With nine people, there would be several spots found, not one. I've discounted this totally because there are no photographs or detailed description related to distance, amount, etc.

Blood. No blood was found around the tent or on the tent. At that time, blood was not as easy to detect as it is now, but considering the circumstances, blood would have been noticed.

There were no other signs or prints of anyone else near the tent.

Based on the evidence and what DA Roberts would look for immediately, it's clear that there was no one else there the night of the tragedy. Seven strong, fit men would have fought back if attacked. No blood means no altercation.

The contents of the tent were listed, but the owners of some items were never even identified. No photograph of the interior items exists. No photograph of the items outside the opening of the tent flap exists.

There were no burns or smoke damage found in relation to the tent. The heater was not in use.

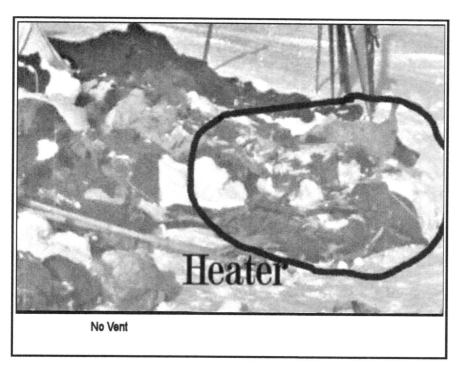

No Vent

Wind: There are severe winds in that area. Some have been reported to be so strong they knock people to the ground. In the diaries, Igor makes special notes of wind conditions because the wind was blowing hard several different times. The last photograph of the tourists alive clearly shows that the wind was blowing the snow.

Hammock said:

Its like a double-edged sword. (...) The wind can also give you anxiety if it's dark (outside).

Cedar tree: This is where some of the worst mistakes occurred.

Roberts:

I would look at burn patterns, cut marks, possible fibers from clothing or hair/fur samples for DNA testing. Also, I would look for possible messages or trail indicators carved by the victims.

First, as soon as the bodies were discovered, the scene should have been secured, measured, and photographed extensively before the bodies were touched.

As far as burn patterns, witness testimony shows discrepancies as to whether the tree had burn marks. If so, where are the photos and careful measurements?

More discrepancies exist as far as the cut marks in the tree. Some reports claim that there were knife cuts; others say branches were broken. Photos and evidence indicate both. But how high the breaks or cuts rose and how many is unclear.

As to the firewood, again, no photographs of the supposed limbs around the fire or other twigs and branches that searchers claimed they saw exist.

How far were the bodies from the tree? If their burned appendages were still close enough to the fire to still burn, that suggests the men died alone, one scenario. But the evidence shows that two, large, heavy men were moved far *away* from the fire. There were no pictures and no measurements taken. Instead, reports were "a few meters". Why are there no clear measurements of the distance between the fire and the tree? The bodies from the tree? The bodies from the fire?

I would look for possible messages or trail indicators carved by the victims. This unusual comment by DA Roberts begs more questions. Did the searchers look for trail indicators or was that evidence accidentally destroyed? If the group separated for any purpose, it stands to reason that they would leave something to show the way to the other group. If they felt as if they would die, why wouldn't they leave something to indicate what had happened and where they were going? (to the ravine). That leads me to believe that, even after the deaths of two to three members of the group, the others didn't expect to die or to need to be rescued.

Searchers said the area around the tree and fire was compacted and full of footprints, but there are no photographs or detailed descriptions. How many footprints were there and to whom did they belong?

There was no evidence of paradoxical undressing; Yuri's and Georgy's clothing were cut off. Clearly, taking the clothing was an attempt to stay warm and to use what was available. It was not disrespectful, but understandable among Siberians. Some clothing was found with the other people in the ravine or along way.

Cut. The clothing was CUT OFF. That evidence makes it clear again that at least one of the group members had a sharp knife.

Georgy had been moved to cut away some of his clothing, explaining why his body was moved after death. No mystery. Burned toes and other areas (hair) specify that frostbite was severe. Foamy spittle is part of pulmonary edema caused by hypothermia. Obviously, both men died of hypothermia; they were the worst dressed for the conditions. The autopsy reports confirm this.

I asked DA Roberts about the knuckle injuries.

Attempting to cut up or break wood for a fire without proper tools could leave wounds on the hands. Also, when the flesh becomes nearly frozen, it becomes brittle and can break and/or cut easily.

This is true. Flesh becomes like weak ice and can be abraded easily. Some branches were broken from the cedar tree. In the best situations, a person's skin would have been ruined, but with frozen hands, it was a given that the knuckles would be injured.

After having enhanced the autopsy photos, I feel that the wounds are consistent with injuries from building *the labaz* and from gathering branches and breaking them. This also explains the bit of flesh found against the bark of the tree. Where is that flesh? How was it collected? Or *was* it collected?

Another piece of evidence comes from what was not found.

I would check for stomach contents and blood pathogens. I would also study the wound patterns, looking for defensive wounds versus animal attack evidence.

What does Roberts mean? He means that the stomach contents are always revealing. In this case, the contents proved that the tourists all died six to eight hours after eating. Because there was no fire the night of February 1 and because the heater was not constructed (recall it took about an hour and half to set it up), the group could not have eaten. Something happened between setting up the tent and getting the heater in place drinks. There is a window of no more than thirty minutes.

Blood and urine are vital. Tests results showed no alcohol was present. It is unknown what drug tests were available in Russia in 1959 and if any tests were done, but the pathologist didn't mention any suspicions.

What wound patterns were there? All members had 4th degree frostbitten fingers, hands, toes, and feet, explained because by the weather. Abrasions were on the faces, arms, hands, explained by their building the *labaz* and their gathering firewood, along with the frozen snow, rocks, and ice. Pulmonary edema and death were explained by hypothermia. The head injuries and broken ribs were caused by massive falls, at least three rocky ridges rose between the slope and cedar tree. The ravine was very deep and filled with rocks and boulders as well.

"Defensive wounds" are found on the palms and forearms when a victim attempts to protect himself. There were none on the nine victims. Neither were there any bite marks that a wild animal would leave nor deep scratches.

The evidence close to the tree was not preserved. With evidence I found and viewed and a logical sequencing, the events at the cedar tree is correct.

It is important to understand that once at the tree, the group knew that, on some level, they were in deep trouble.

When a goal is threatened, a positive attitude can quickly turn into a negative attitude. You may think about all the time, effort, and energy spent training for a certain goal is wasted. The negative emotions could sway a person to give up on the task at hand. (Brad Hammock)

The Slope: Immediately after they left the tent, they walked away as a group. Reports declared six to ten sets of footprints, depending on various interviews. Nine sets would be logical and follow the evidence of the few pictures taken. No measurements were added, and no flags set. The prints were lost.

With poor weather conditions, freezing temperatures, fear, worry, and exhaustion, and with little-to-no-light, there is no possible way that the tourists did not fall more than once. The non-working flashlight was located below the last ridge.

Rustik is the wild card. Most don't believe he died first, but he had to. Had he made it to the ravine and hit his head there, he couldn't have crawled so far back up the slope; his injury was severe. Same for the tree.

Had he travelled to the ravine, not been unhurt, and decided to return to the tent, he would have taken their boots to wear if Semyon and Kolya were dead. He didn't, so he was not at the ravine after they were dead. If they were alive and he were at the ravine, there would be no logical reason for him to leave them, and without shoes, try to crawl to the tent.

According to the autopsy report, he did have a serious head wound and was found on the slope; therefore, it was impossible that he ever made it to the fire or to the ravine. The only place he could have hit his head that badly was on the ridge(s). Logically, he had to have hit his head before the others reached the cedar or ravine. He died of hypothermia and the head wound.

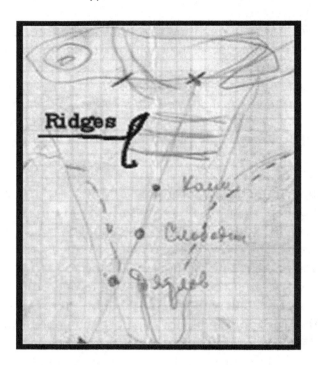

Another clue is that he was the only one who was warm enough to melt the snow when he died. It's the only timeline that fits the obvious evidence. Many seem to see Rustik as a very brave athlete (which he was) and wish to believe that he suffered terribly but still managed to crawl back along the slope.

Unfortunately, because of his body temperature and head wound, it's clear that he died first.

Somewhere on the stone ridge, Slobodin trips and smashes his head and soon falls.

The tent is not visible anymore, legs burn from the cold snow, and maybe Slobodin falls at the end of the group of fugitives,

and remains lying on the snow. And somewhere even earlier, Zina Kolmogorova lost sight of the group. After wondering for a long time, she also lies down on the snow. The rest reach the forest, in the deep snow and begin with inhuman efforts to fight for life.
(Akselrod Moses Abramovich, searcher)

I concede that it might look possible that Igor and Zina died on the slope before reaching the cedar tree. If so, they had to have been walking back to the tent based on forensics photographs. They died facing the direction of the tent, and their lower body positions indicate they were climbing.

This is impossible. Both had wounds consistent with injuries acquired from breaking branches and gathering wood with freezing hands. But neither had head wounds.

Zina had extra clothing she took from Yuri, removed *after* his death.

Zina and Igor went to the tree with Yuri, Georgy, and the others. Because Igor wasn't one to leave the rest of his team behind, he and Zina walked to the ravine with the others, minus Rustik, Yuri, and Georgy.

They had no reason to go back a mile to the tent; their goal would have been to make a shelter or a den, start a warm fire, and wait for the morning. They all must have reached the ravine between 10:45 and 11:30. Dawn was about seven-eight hours away.

After the tragedy in the ravine and fully demoralized, exhausted, and freezing, Igor started back to the tent. The weather had cleared. He didn't have a compass, yet he took a direct path back to the tent; he could *see* it. He fell and died of hypothermia.

Zina followed, found his body, and turned him over, maybe to get more warm clothing, but her fingers were frozen. She continued walking and died of hypothermia.

The Ravine: Theorists swarm to this case because of those found in the ravine and their terrible injuries as compared to the other tourists' injuries. The pathologist said that the injuries were consistent with having been hit by a car. They weren't.

Lyuda was found on the very boulder that she fell upon. She broke her ribs, and one of the broken ribs punctured her heart. Her violent injuries and hypothermia caused death. When she fell, she bit off a part of her tongue. The report stated that her tongue was missing, not ripped out. Not cut off. *Missing*.

When Kolya fell, he hit his head and sustained massive, fatal head injuries.

Semyon, unable to catch himself as he fell, broke his ribs, accelerating the hypothermia, causing his death.

Sasha had a deep cut on the side/back of his head. It wasn't fatal, but hypothermia was.

Exposure, severe decomposition, running water, possibly animals or birds, and the weather explain the loss of facial and body flesh and the missing eyes of those down in the ravine

According to Roberts:

Every scene is a potential crime scene. Even accidental or natural causes. Until foul play can be eliminated completely, every scene must be contained and treated as a crime scene. Things like blood splatter, defensive wounds, toxins and unexplained wounds. Of course, there are other significant indicators like witness interviews or conflicting stories.

Again, even accidental/natural deaths are still treated as a crime scene until its proven that they aren't. The presence or lack of defensive wounds is a big one. Any unattended death is automatically investigated as a crime scene. It has to be. You can tell a vast difference in blunt force trauma from a car wreck versus damage from a club or baseball bat. There are dozens of subtle indicators that can give away the origin of wounds or cause of death.

Unfortunately, the crime scene was never secured. Almost three months passed before every victim was located. Huge numbers of searchers trampled the area. At some point, there was an investigation in the form of interviewing witnesses.

The knife: The fourth knife is either still out there and can't be found because no one is sure where the ravine is, or the knife was taken by a searcher.

When the case was closed on May 28, the official ruling was death because of "*a compelling force*". The compelling force was nature.

Part V

Incorrect Evidence/ Folktales

- Lyuda's tongue was cut out: It wasn't. It was missing. The autopsy doesn't say how much of her tongue was missing or the causation. It's logical that she bit part of it off when she fell, and decomposition caused the rest. Her face was so terribly decomposed that when her father saw her, he fainted.
- Lyuda was strangled to death: Her hyoid bone was intact. One or both hyoid horns break when a person is strangled.
- Sasha was strangled to death: Hyoid bone intact. His neck was described as *deformed* in the autopsy report, not broken hyoid bone nor broken neck. He could have died from any manner of injury such as that of a fall when he hit the back of his head on a rock in the ravine.
- Eyes were cut out: The eye loss is because to birds and decomposition.
- A fall could not have caused the severe rib breaks: Yes, it could and did. Falling from several yards directly onto a boulder causes breaks.
- A fall would have broken other bones: Not if the impact were directly on the chest or head. A falling person doesn't always reach out to stop the impact. Absence of other breaks doesn't mean anything other than the fall was sudden and massive.
- There was a huge amount of radiation discovered: By modern standards, the amount was within limits. Three

of the men had worked in fields that caused radioactive dust. Had there been something very radioactive, it would have been found all over every victim. It was found on only a few items.

- The bodies and tent were posed: No, but some of the injured were moved by the others to try to relieve their pain and to gather their clothing. Maybe to checked for vital signs. The tent was set up correctly, but the wind shifted and caused snow drifts at the entrance.

- Everyone had head wounds: Kolya had a fatal head fracture. Rustik had a severe head injury. Sasha had a minor wound that was on his scalp but was deepened by decomposition.

- Lyuda and Semyon were beaten and their ribs broken: Facial wounds are inconsistent with being beaten. They had bruises and abrasions consistent with the conditions and then a serious fall into the ravine.

- Sasha and Igor committed suicide: There is no proof. If anything, they began suffering paradoxical undressing.

- Some had brick-orange skin: Possible mummification. Decomposition. Weathering in the altitude.

- They would never have panicked enough to leave the tent: Hypoxia can cause that. Panic spreads panic. Half dressed, they left the tent which implies that they didn't expect to be outside long. Increasing wind and a storm would drive them out to make a fire at the tree line, afraid to return to the tent.

- Rustik was beaten and injured at the tent and was carried by the others: It's far more likely and simple to assume that he was injured by falling on one of the ridges. Although he was athletic, that doesn't eliminate the fact that he likely fell and hit his head. He died on the slope without reaching the fire at the tree, evidenced by the melted snow from his body heat and his "corpse bed".

- Rustik and Igor had a fight: Their hands do not support that. The abrasions are minor, and the same kinds of injuries were found on others, particularly Zina. The wounds are not consistent with a fist fight and were not cited as such by the coroner.

- Semyon and Kolya did not stay with the others when they all ran out of the tent: The footprints suggest that someone veered to the side for a few yards but then returned. In tracking their friends, it's unlikely they would leave the trail. If they were together, someone could have veered to the side to look around for ridges or creeks to avoid.

- They ate their evening meal: Autopsy reports show that they ate six to eight hours before death. If they ate, then whatever happened, occurred about 3:00 am or later which is possible, except that would be the first night to miss a group journal entry. It would also imply they built a firepit with plenty of wood, cooked their meal in blizzard conditions, cleaned up, constructed the heater and set ups the vents and thus slept in the warm tent without having to put on extra clothing. There was no firepit built nor firewood available. There were no journal entries written for that date. The heater was disassembled, and the vents were not in place. They were not wearing their tent shoes, and their blankets were still bunched up. They never went to sleep. Whatever happened was immediately after setting up the tent. Photos of them during set-up are an hour or maybe less before death.

- The coroner was inept: For that time period, he was qualified and did as well as he could. By modern standards, a lot of information is missing such as details, measurements, opinions, and photographs. Because some information is missing, many people add their own information to fit theories; this is breaking the rules of evidence gathering. Personal details must not be added, nor any findings dismissed but must follow the autopsy findings to the proper theories.

- The women were raped: The autopsy clearly says that neither was sexually active, and their clothing does not suggest this.

- The tourists were drunk: The autopsy results say clearly that alcohol was not present. No one was drunk.

- The urine amount for each person makes no sense: In those with little urine, the answer is that they urinated before death. Igor had a higher level of urine. As he was going through hypothermia, his body, in order to preserve itself, refused to relax and allow him to urinate; it was probably painful. The fact that after death, he still didn't release the urine because it was found in his bladder proves that he froze quickly.

- The Mansi killed them. The Mansi killed a female geologist after tying her hands and feet and throwing her into a lake for daring to go "where women shouldn't go". Unsubstantiated.

- Georgy was a spy and contacted his operatives when he was arrested: He had no information to pass on at that time. If he were involved in a nefarious plan, he would have dressed warmly to carry it out, and yet he was one of the most poorly dressed for the weather conditions. This accusation pops up at times, but there is no proof and seems to be the idea of would-be sleuths that believe a complicated, unsubstantiated idea must be the answer. This is an embarrassment to those who suggest it.

- The tent was slashed from the inside during a panic: First, the footsteps indicate hurried movements to get away from the tent, and a fast get-away, but not panic. I don't agree that it was cut from the inside. The three knives were found sheathed. The fourth sheath and cuts on branches show there was a fourth Finnish knife, and the logical owner was a former military man, Semyon. It is very possible that one of the searchers used a knife to slash the tent open while others used a shovel and ice axe. One piece of evidence that is critical is that *not one searcher described snow inside the tent*; they said they saw clothing, journals, the knives, food, and a cup of cocoa, but they never mentioned snow. *Wouldn't snow enter through a floor to ceiling gash in the tent?* I think that Semyon cut the tent from the outside or *that a searcher cut it,* and I lean toward the latter.
- The fire by the cedar was not made by the tourists but was the remains of and older one: A bit of a coincidence. Yuri and Georgy died beside that fire and they had burns.
- The burns were from torture or the stove: Torture by fire involves increasing areas. It's ridiculous to imagine a leg, a toe, or hair burned at random. It isn't very torturous to burn people when their appendages are frozen, and they can't feel pain.

- A searcher found a notebook and pen in Semyon's possession, found nothing written, and tossed them away: Unsubstantiated.
- The notebook was staged: Why? Unsubstantiated and unbelievable.
- Sasha was a spy and knew secrets about nuclear power, and an assassination team came after him. There's nothing to suggest that he was. If there were an assassination team, they were stealthy in terms of not leaving any evidence, but inept in every other way. Their ways of killing witnesses was sloppy and complicated (waiting while a few freeze). They must have had no animosity because other than his head injury, Sasha wasn't physically assaulted. And they didn't bother to make the bodies vanish? Seems very far-fetched in every way possible.
- CPR broke their ribs: Rib 2 is difficult to break because it lies under the collar bone. Forensics showed that the rib breakage occurred when the victims were alive and were broken in one event.
- Sasha was hit by a gun: Evidence? None.
- The tourists were tied with ropes: This is inconsistent with injuries. Their hands were raised to preserve warmth as they fell and died. Those with hands raised probably experienced the strange phenomenon of flushing and feeling hot while freezing to death. *Besides, to subdue a person, the hands are tied behind their backs.*
- The "device" mentioned in a diary was a... (pick any mysterious object): The device was a thermometer, and

that was part of the group's goal: to measure soil temperatures.

- Snow around the tent was intentionally disguised: Or the tourists walked over it a lot as they set up camp and/or searchers tracked down the snow, ruining any possible evidence.
- Lyuda's stomach was full of blood: It wasn't according to the autopsy. It shows she swallowed some blood which would have been the case if she had bitten off part of her tongue.
- They all vomited blood: They didn't. Some had a bloody or brown foam on their lips, from pulmonary edema due to hypothermia. Bloody noses were caused from falling on freezing faces.
- A rocket exploded: Supposedly it was cleaned up secretly and quickly, or the remains of the rocket may still be there. If parts are ever found, even if they are from a downed rocket from 1980, the rocket theorists will remain steadfast.
- The footprints show that they were forced to stand in a line of nine: The photographed footprints are not consistent with this. Zero evidence exists.
- A strange foot print of a heeled boot shows that there were intruders: Semyon's boot had a heel.
- No bruising means it was a ray gun: No. A lack of bruising indicates that the tourists were freezing. They fell, broke their bones, and died within minutes of freezing. There was no time for bruising to occur.
- Several fell out of the tree, killing them: If people don't believe that a fall into a rocky ravine couldn't break the ribs of Lyuda and Semyon and cause Sasha's and Kolya's

head injuries (or Rustik's), then how would a fall from the tree onto the snow-covered ground cause the injuries? If they did fall from the tree and receive those injuries, there would be no one left to make the den, much to less to travel.

- The clothing proves nothing: It proves a timeline. It proves that there was a knife in use (other than a small pocket knife). It proves that the bodies were moved after death as supported by forensics. It proves that the group members did everything possible to stay alive. As soon as clothing is discounted or the evidence is altered in regard to it, any following theory should be ignored.
- There were eleven bodies recovered: Unsubstantiated.

Part VI

Dispelling Other Theories

According to DA Roberts:

Too many investigators go into a scene with preconceived theories can pollute your investigation. You must collect the evidence to form your theories, not seek evidence that supports your theory.

Memories are fallible. Time changes our perceptions. The more time between interviews with the witnesses, the more likely that their recollection has changed. Your far more likely to get better testimony immediately after the incident than you will days later. Or in the case of the Dyatlov Pass incident, decades later.

Theories are listed in no order. Each is given a star rating.
One star is ludicrous, and there is zero evidence to support the theory.
Two stars is interesting but doesn't fit the evidence.
Three stars is a remote possibility but highly unlikely and inconsistent with the evidence.
Four stars is possible but....
Five stars is very likely.

***** My theory: It fits the evidence.

*Yeti: The satirical newspaper that the tourists wrote fueled this theory, and a photo was used to "prove it". Yetis, if they are real, are likely to be white to blend in. The arms look like a man's arm.

Enhanced to show there is a sweater and pants

Enhanced to show there is a sweater and pants

This enhanced photo shows a lot. The arms are not those of a yeti. Pants bloom over a boot and are tucked in. This is someone thin. The person is wearing a ski mask. This person is also wearing a sweater. He had come out from behind a tree, probably after relieving himself. Had this been a real Yeti, no doubt someone would have mentioned the fact in the group (or a personal) diary. No. There were no claw or bite marks.

(Also called a snowman or a menk)

Fly Agaric: It is possible that the tourists experimented with this mushroom that causes hallucinations. Igor and the others were level-headed. They tried to avoid cigarettes, took no alcohol (but a flask of medicinal vodka). Igor, Rustik, and Sasha would not have tried this when they needed to finish setting up the tent and blankets and had to set up the heater.

Brad Hammock, experienced mountaineer, especially at the 10K range explained in a way that leads me to believe that the group didn't need drugs.

It's (hiking/summiting) the feeling of conquering the world, the sunrise views, the clouds, no worries, and pure bliss.

Mansi natives attacked: They were interviewed as were witnesses. Never had they attacked mountaineers. Had they been the culprits, it's likely the tourists' possessions would have been stolen.

Khanty-Mansia (Mansi) hunt in lower altitudes but not where the Dyatlov Nine were.

While it's true that their skis would not leave many prints, it is logical to believe that there would be, at least, a *few* ski trails.

The camp was not in an area (Kholat Sykhal) considered to be holy.

Several Mansi were interrogated, but the theory didn't fit the evidence.

The mountain where the tent and the dead bodies were found is not a Mansi sacred place. Mansi sacred places are very far from there. While Stepan Kurikov and other Mansi helped with the search, their behavior was normal, and they even regretted that what happened to the tourists was so bad. What I saw and the circumstances under which they died, I can only assume that they perish from the elements. Mansi should not be prosecuted for the death of the tourists. The group of tourists could have frozen because of a hurricane that tore the tent and broke loose and they try to fix it or even managed to do that before being blown by the wind and dragged in the ravine, where they lost orientation and couldn't get back to the tent and died from the cold. I have nothing more to add. (Al. Cheglakov)

***Avalanche:** This theory rates three stars only because the noise of the wind and thunder could have caused the group to *believe* there was about to be an avalanche and thus, left the tent in a near panic.

The area was not steep enough, less than a twenty-degree slope.

The tent was not covered by snow nor were the poles dislodged.

Footprints were present.

Those fleeing from a possible avalanche would not walk in the straight line down the slope. They would move out of the potential path.

If the tent were partially covered, they would have dug away the snow. Shelter. The heater and warm clothing were in the tent; they would not retreat and doom themselves because of an event they could rectify.

The skis, used with ropes to hold the tent up, were found standing straight.

Theorists generally cite two ways this could happen. 1. Lyuda, Rustik, Kolya, and Semyon were hurt by the avalanche and carried to the ravine. Why not dig out the tent and care for them? Lyuda, Kolya, and Semyon were far too injured to be carried a mile by freezing friends. Also, the footprints disprove this. 2. The avalanche carried them a mile and battered those with violent injuries into the ravine. Impossible. Again, footprints.

Hammock summed it:

"Footprints leading out of the tent were not covered with snow. No trees were uprooted or broken in half. The tent should've been demolished."

*UFO: A random photo sparked this theory.

There is no evidence. Reports of glowing lights by witnesses cite instances *after* February 1. One investigator was fascinated with UFOs and said:

> When E. P. Maslennikov and I examined the scene in May, we found that some young pine trees at the edge of the forest had burn marks, but those marks did not have a concentric form or some other pattern. There was no epicenter. This once again confirmed that heated beams of a strong, but completely unknown, at least to us, energy, were directing their firepower toward specific objects (in this case, people), acting selectively.

> On February 17, 1959, at 6 o'clock (illegible) minutes of the morning, I was on duty.
> At this time, from the south side, appeared a ball of large sizes, enveloped in white fog. The big circle. When moving across the sky, the ball then increased, then decreased its brightness. With a decrease, the ball hid in a white fog, and only a luminous dot could be seen through this fog. Periodically the luminous point increased its brightness, increasing also in size. With increasing brightness, the luminous point, which took the form of a sphere, it seemed to push the fog (unintelligible), while at the same time increasing its density along the edges, and then hiding itself in the fog. The impression was created that the ball itself radiated this (inaudible) fog, which formed the shape of a circle around (inaudible). The ball moved very slowly and at high altitude. This ball was visible for ten minutes, and then disappeared in the north, as if melted away. That's all I saw.
> I personally wrote the interrogation protocol
> April 7, 1959. A. L. Anisimov (signature)
> Jr Prosecutor Ivdel Tempalov (signature)

Some garments (from the ravine) tested positive for radiation. It was not very strong, and three of the men had worked in nuclear fields around radiation. It's likely their clothing absorbed the radiation. A UFO would have probably left radiation on all the tourists and all over them, not on waist bands only.

17 III To Tempalov from K. Piguzov
16. III.59
To the Chief of the Ivdel Police Station 17. II. 59, 6 h. 50 m. local time in the sky appeared not unnatural phenomenon. Moving star with a tail. The tail looked like dense cirrus clouds. Then the star was freed from the tail, became brighter than the stars, and flew away. It gradually began to swell, forming a large ball, enveloped in a haze. Then inside this ball, the star caught fire, from which first a crescent was formed, then a small ball formed, not so bright. The big ball gradually began to fade, became like a blurry spot. At 7 h. 05 m. it disappeared altogether. A star moved from the south to the northeast.

Meteorological technician Tokareva (signature)
Chief GMS Piguzova (signature)

Conclusion
Samples of solid biosubstrates and clothes combined in groups under Nos 1, 2, 3,4 were submitted to the radio-isotope laboratory of the Sverdlovsk sanitary epidemic station and were analyzed for presence of radioactive materials.
Dosimetric measurements of clothes showed excessive radioactivity (Betaemission only, no Alpha or Gamma-quanta) of 200–300 counts per minute (cpm) over the natural background. Further investigation allowed maximum contamination to be established on different spots of clothing:

Brown sweater from №4: 9900 cpm on 150 cm²
Bottom part of bloomers from №1: 5000 cpm on 150   cm²
Belt of sweater from №1: 5600 cpm on 150 cm²
(Signature of Levashov)

While they might have watched a UFO and wondered about it, it's doubtful that they would have left in a hurry, took nothing with them, braved the subzero temperatures, and retreated a mile.

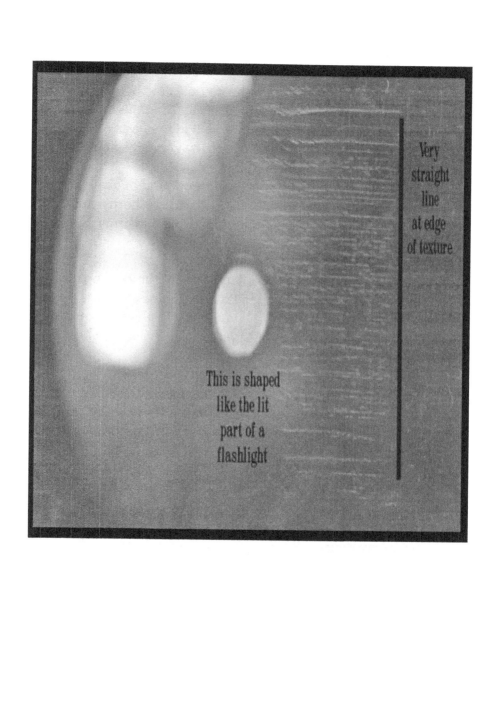

*The Stove: I have covered this, and the evidence is clear that it was never used. The stomach contents and photos support this. No smoke or fire damage. Yes, a jacket was burned by the heater, but that was mentioned in the diaries, days before the fatal night. It wasn't used and disassembled, either, and this is known because of stomach contents. In addition, had they assembled the heater, they would have kept it going to stay warm. Logic.

The stove was located approximately in the middle of the tent in a disassembled state in its case. (Chernyshov Aleksey Alekseevich, assistant Chief of Staff in army unit 6602 in charge of the training)

*Ball lightning: While this might account for glowing orbs and the panic to leave the tent, it falls apart. Some theorists believe it caused the burns of Yuri and Georgy (highly improbable), then caused the injuries to Lyuda, Semyon, Kolya, and maybe Rustik. Maybe Sasha. It left no burns on them.

The theory suggests the ball lightning struck near the tent, causing them to evacuate, followed them a mile, after about two hours and struck again, killing Yuri and Georgy, then, about two hours later, followed them to the ravine and killed four more. It injured Rustik. The ball lightning didn't care about harming Zina and Igor.

Reports of glowing orbs or ball lightning don't coincide with the date.

*Teleportation: This is based on an awful movie, and I refuse to waste time refuting this idea. Ridiculous.

****Hypoxia: At 10K, Hypoxia isn't expected, but it is more than possible. It could explain why so many hikers make unexpected, strange choices that make no sense at all.

At 10K, there is a 30 percent loss of oxygen. Headaches, anxiety, hallucinations, confusion, and disorientation are the first symptoms (Confirmed by Hammock, this theory was the first he listed on possibilities).

There have been many cases when groups at high altitudes split up, randomly climbed higher and died, wandered around, screamed, and made choices that led to death.

*A Death ray: Odd theory. Where did it come from? Did the Russian try it as an experiment? Was someone holding it but not leaving tracks? If this is true, it wasn't very impressive since only Kolya was killed outright by a head injury. Rustik could have been saved. Lyuda and Semyon were hurt badly but not killed at once. The rest didn't get the force of the death ray; someone must have had it out for Lyuda, Kolya, and Semyon only.

***Infrasound: this is more possible. Certain sounds made by the wind can cause anxiety, nausea, poor decision-making skills, panic, and fear. Coming down along each side of the hill, the noise would be impressive. Before it is consciously heard by humans, it is heard subconsciously. A low frequency sound, it affects about a fifth of the population.

Only one or two would be affected and cause them to flee the tent.

Wouldn't the others have dressed warmly before chasing after their friends?

Whether it could last long enough to cause them to leave their shelter and supplies is unknown. I do think there were terrifying noises from the storm (thunder and roaring), but the infrasound theory possibly adds to the why the tourists flew the tent.

*Hikers mistaken for escaped convicts: Although there was a *gulag* a few miles away, no escapes were reported, so no one would be looking for escapees. A bunch of kids camping on the hill could not be mistaken for a group of escaped prisoners.

Since there were no escapes and no signs of human violence, this theory as well as the one that surmised that escapees killed the group can be eliminated.

*Semyon was a spy: He joined the group late. He was older, unmarried, and former military. Supposedly, he ordered everyone out of the tent at knife-point. No one attempted to overtake him, and he followed them down the slope. He hit Zina in her back with a baton (Not found), leaving a bruise. He hit Rustik and left his body. At the tree, although he wanted them dead, he allowed them to use his knife to cut branches. (outrageous idea) He let Yuri and Georgy freeze but allows someone to cut off the clothing or does it himself.

Next, he gets everyone to the ravine. Zina and Igor escape and die on the slope.

He allows the others to gather branches.

Either Lyuda and Kolya fall into the ravine to die, or he pushes them; he doesn't stab them. Finally, he hits Sasha on the back of his head to kill him and hurts Sasha's neck.

Finally, Semyon falls to *his* death in the ravine but manages to get rid of his Finnish knife and the baton or stick.

When he is found, he holds his journal and a pencil which is remarkable for a man who is dying. Someone rips it away because there is nothing written, and it's forgotten.

He is found with a camera case. Supposedly there was an unbroken camera and ruined film.

*Ergot: The tourists purchased bread in the last camp they were in. Ergot poisoning causes irrational behavior and thoughts (Salem witch trials). Maybe that's why everyone exited the tent, and someone cut it. It could explain a few parts of the case, but the group was rational at the cedar tree and fire, able to get branches, able to gather clothing after their friends died, able to make a snow den, and able to gather more wood. Did hallucinations return and cause several to fling themselves off the ravine and to their deaths? Did they only become coherent at the tree but not anywhere else on the one-mile trek *to* the tree? That's very selective.

The woodcutters didn't report any adverse effects from eating their bread.

No evidence is available to support such a theory.

*Tetanus: Several members scratched their hand on nails at the last camp. No doubt they were rusted nails. Symptoms may include urine retention and anxiety. Could all nine suddenly feel the symptoms all at once? Did they run out to save someone who was showing symptoms? The footprints don't indicate this. Hypothermia also caused urine retention; those with low urine in their bladders might have relieved themselves before the event.

This is a shot in the dark and doesn't fit any evidence whatsoever.

*KGB: Of course, people want to blame the KGB. They were meeting Sasha or Semyon to obtain secrets. Semyon had tattoos, and one had never been translated. (DAERMMUAZUAYA). Some had worked in nuclear facilities and might be about to share secrets. They had to be stopped. They even had proof of radiation on some clothing.

An addition is that American CIA were also there. It's good to spread the blame. The KGB and CIA sent the tourists into brutal conditions to kill them, then tossed several into a ravine to kill them, hit Sasha with the butt of a gun, and vanished.

They left no footprints on the slope alongside the group and mysteriously knew where to find them even after Igor changed the course. Maybe Igor was part of the plot. Georgy worked in a nuclear capacity at one point and must be added to the traitors.

That is sloppy if both organizations didn't bother to stage the crime scenes or dispose of the bodies or get the radioactive clothing.

It's far too convoluted and messy and fits zero evidence.

*Missiles: Possible but not probable.

RADIOGRAM TO SULMAN
3/2-59 yr. — 18:30
[…] the main mystery of the tragedy remains the exit
of the entire group out of the tent […]
The reason could be any extraordinary natural
phenomenon, such as the flight of a meteorological
rocket.

Locals describe a military presence in the area.

Where are the remains of a rocket that exploded and scared the group from the tent? Why didn't they take clothing? Why did they leave the tent to begin with?

This goes back to an earlier theory that is clear regarding why people could not be injured at the tent and fails to explain (another rocket) the ravine occurrence. Did the rocket explode there, tossing them into the ravine and making a few bits of clothing radioactive?

Again, like the ball lightning, it's improbable that rockets chased them.

*A meteor: See above.

*Testing: For what? What was tested by the military on nine mountaineers? How long it takes to freeze? Zero evidence.

*Skin Color due to radiation: Some said that a few had brick orange colored skin. They had wind and sun burn. Exposure changes skin color at higher altitudes after death. Bodies left on Mount Everest show the same odd colors at times. At least four of the bodies were very decomposed.

It's also very likely that the person who prepared the bodies used make-up to cover the worst of the wounds and to off-set the *pallor mortis*, paleness of death.

****High Winds: A freak wind could have blown down the sides of the hill, terrifying the group with the noises. It might come in bursts. During the rescue, one witness said:

Strong winds constantly blow on the investigated slopes and along the valley, usually at a speed of 15-20 m/s, often reaching up to 36 m/s and more (according to weather service). People can barely overcome the power of the wind. If it snows a storm starts, in which visibility is reduced to 3-5 m. Storms are frequent here in the last days of February and early March. For example, from March 5, the weather is sunny, the snowstorm are only at the basis of the snow being drifted, but ice crust started to form on the entire surface of the slopes and causing frequent falls. On March 9, a Soloviev soldier from Potapov group fel,l and his trauma doesn't allow him to move.

"Gale force winds 50-150mph, maybe up to 300mph. Gravity is reduced which makes winds stronger. I've been in 60-80mph winds at 12k." (Brad Hammock)

(Rempel Ivan Dmitrievich, Forester of Vizhay Forestry) *The witness testified: on January 25, 1959, a group of tourists addressed me as the head of the forestry, they showed me their route seeking advice what is the best way to get to Mt Otorten and asked me to familiarize them with our maps of the area where they are going. When I got acquainted with their route, I expressed my opinion that in wintertime it is dangerous to go along the Ural ridge because there are large gorges, pits in which you can fall and besides there are strong winds raging, people have been hurt. I told them my concern because I know this area of the Ural range from the words of local resident, I myself have not been there.*

*Murderer among the group: This implies that everyone left everything behind and didn't try to overcome the attacker. Rustik, Sasha, Lyuda, Semyon, and Kolya died violently, and the killer wouldn't have been underdressed, so the other four are immediately eliminated as the killer.

Second scenario is the killer was one who died violently and by accident. He would be dressed well. Semyon and Kolya are the only two who fit. Kolya should be eliminated by profiling. After seeing their friends killed, as a large group, they attacked and killed Semyon, or if some had already fallen and died, the remaining trio attacked: Zina, Sasha, and Igor. Ignoring his weapon, they beat him to death but only on one side of his chest. Sasha felt bad about killing him and lay down next to Semyon to die. That makes no sense.

** Semyon again: Semyon pushed some into the ravine (no one fought back because his face and hands don't show expected wounds), allowed some to freeze, then fell accidentally, and was killed. It begs the question of why no one fought back. What motive would he have? Did he expect to survive on his own? Have an extraction plan? Plan to defect?

It's just far too messy and unsubstantiated. For this to have happened, a very convoluted timeline would be needed. The evidence would be looked at in opposite ways, and an entire backstory would be constructed.

Had he wished to defect and leave the others behind, he could have waited for the summit, and there was no reason to chance killing them except to give himself more time to escape; there is no proof that shows he desired to defect.

He had no reason to murder the other eight. Unless he had to kill them because they saw something that was top secret, they didn't have to die. If someone higher up had predicted the group *might* see something, why not just deny them permission to go and stop them from seeing anything to begin with?

Maybe he alone tried fly agaric or had ergot poisoning. Maybe he went stark raving mad for some unknown reason. Maybe the noises only affected him. It's all unlikely.

*Serial killers: Two or three spree killers either tracked the group or came across them. There is no evidence of killers at the tent; thus, there were no killers to lure the group out of the tent and down a mile slope.

If there were killers, they would have set up a den in the ravine. (In the dark so the group was not alerted by the lights) Next, they would have made a fire by the cedar tree, attracting the tourists

The theoretical killers would not have bothered to shoot or stab the Dyatlov members but would have allowed the two to freeze to death after they had gathered more wood. (Rustik may or may not have been alive).

After an hour and a half, the killers would have put out the fire, allowed someone to borrow a knife and cut away some warmer clothing, and then they would have gone to the ravine for some unknown reason. Once there, either several of the tourists would have fallen to their deaths in the ravine or would have been murdered. Zina, Igor, and maybe Rustik escaped, but they would have died on the way back to the tent.

Bindings are not substantiated by scrapes and cuts. Marks on a few of the victims' legs are clearly from the bindings they used on the boot covers.

*Mysterious sudden force: This is a theory that suggests a force but gives no explanation. This idea doesn't explain the tent exit or any other events but is focused on the deaths in the ravine. Witnesses report the ravine was twelve to twenty-four feet high. No one agrees. No one is positive where the ravine was because it's now impossible to identify after sixty years. The theory is based on the following:

The text of the conclusion of the examination

Question: From what kind of force could Thibeaux-Brignolle have received such injury?
Answer: In the conclusion, it's shown the damage to Thibeaux-Brignolle's head could have been the result of the throwing, fall or jettisoning of the body. I don't believe these wounds could have been the result of Thibeaux-Brignolle simply falling from the level of his own height, i.e. falling and hitting his head. The extensive, depressed, multi-splintered (broken fornix and base of the skull) fracture could be the result of an impact of an automobile moving at high speed. This kind of trauma could have occurred if Thibeaux-Brignolle had been thrown and fallen and hit his head against rocks, ice, etc., by a gust of strong wind.
Question: Is it possible that Thibeaux-Brignolle was hit by a rock that was in someone's hand?
Answer: In this case, there would have been damage to the soft tissue, and this was not evident.
Question: How long could Thibeaux-Brignolle have lived after the trauma. Could he have moved on his own, talked, etc.?
Answer: After this trauma, Thibeaux-Brignolle would have had a severe concussion; that is, he would have been in an unconscious state. Moving him would have been difficult and, close to the end, movement would not have been possible. I believe he would not have been able to move even if he had been helped. He could only have been carried or dragged. He could have shown signs of life for 2-3 hours.

Question: How is it possible to explain the cause of the damage to Dubinina and Zolotaryov? Is it possible to combine them into one cause?

Answer: I think the character of the injuries on Dubinina and Zolotaryov – a multiple fracture of the ribs – on Dubinina were bilateral and symmetrical, and on Zolotaryov were one-sided. Both had hemorrhaging into the cardiac muscle with hemorrhaging into the pleural cavity, which is evidence of them being alive [when injured] and is the result of the action of a large force, similar to the example used for Thibeaux-Brignolle. These injuries, especially appearing in such a way without any damage to the soft tissue of the chest, are very similar to the type of trauma that results from the shock wave of a bomb.

Question: How long could Dubinina and Zolotaryov have lived?

Answer: Dubinina died 10-20 minutes after the trauma. She could have been conscious. Sometimes it happens that a person with a wound to the heart (for example, a serious knife wound) can talk, run, and ask for help. Dubinina's situation was one of complicated traumatic shock resulting from the bilateral rib fracture, followed by internal hemorrhaging into the pleural cavity. Zolotaryov could have lived longer. It needs to be taken into account that they were all trained, physically fit, and strong people.

(Vozrozhdenny Boris Alekseevich, forensic expert).

*Igor murder/suicide: Convoluted but interesting. The theory was that Igor was either insane or jealous that Yuri and Zina were rekindling a romance and decided to kill everyone and himself. Grabbing one of the women as a hostage, he took a fourth knife and cut the tent, ordering everyone out quickly. Kolya and Semyon already had stepped out of the tent, so the timing was perfect for the attack. Once outside, he made everyone walk down the slope.

Rustik fought back and so did Zina, causing their abraded knuckles. Rustik and Zina died on the slope. Then, Igor died on the slope. Kolya and Semyon came to the rescue and made a fire at the tree line (They didn't come to the rescue until the others were far from the tent. The merging of footprints doesn't indicate when someone veered back to walk in the same tracks.)

Proponents believe the lines on Igor's ankles weren't from the boot covers but from binding. (If he didn't die on the slope.)

The use of the dead's clothing was ignored. The autopsy reports were ignored.

***Tent was cut from inside:** This doesn't change my theory. It only means that the 4th knife was used from within the tent to escape.

Original analysis:

ACT № 199 forensic expertise
Written on April 16, 1959.
The case of the death of student tourists from Dyatlov group April 3, 1959 from the Prosecutor's Office of Sverdlovsk region under the order of 16 / III-59. criminal prosecutor Jr. Justice Adviser Ivanova L.N. for the production of forensic examination entered the tourist tent of the Dyatlov group, found at the scene.
THE FOLLOWING PROBLEMS ARE ASSIGNED TO THE EXPERTISE:

1. Is Dyatlov group tent cut?

2. If yes, are the cuts made from inside or outside?

The production of this expertise was entrusted to the expert-criminalist Churkina H. E. with a higher legal education and experience as an expert in the field since 1954. (...)
INSPECTION AND INVESTIGATION

(...) To recreate the situation close to the situation of the scene, with the help and advice of the tourist Yudin Y., the tent in question was pitched and reinforced in such a way as it is usually arranged by the hikers when camping. The tent is made of thick cotton fabric of protective color. The total length of the tent /by the top seam/ is 4m.33 cm, the length of the side is 1 m. 14 cm, the total width is about 2 m. The height of the tent depends on its installation. From the left end of the tent, there is a hole that serves as an entrance. This hole is formed by two non-sewn halves of the fabric, and from the inside is creped with a white sheet. From the right end there is a small round hole sewn in the form of a sleeve and intended for ventilation. From the side edges on the tent attached loops with twine, serving to strengthen it. There is no twine at the end of the right skate. The tent is worn down. When inspecting the tent, it is established that on its surface there are numerous damages, especially on the right slant of the canopy forming the roof /see scheme №1/.With a careful examination of these damages, it is established that some of them /and in particular conditionally marked damages №1,2,3/ have a completely different nature compared to all the other damages that are on the tent. The edges of these three lesions have even, not elongated ends of the threads, are damaged at different angles, breaking both the weft threads and the warp threads. All woven items /unlike jersey, leather etc./, despite a sharp difference in appearance /raw material, thickness, surface character/ always consist of 3 systems of threads - warp and weft, interwoven perpendicular to each other. The damage resulting from tears usually follows the line of least resistance, i.e. tear either the threads of the weft, or the warp threads. Such damage is usually very smooth and has right angles. The cut, under any conditions, always disrupts both those and other threads at different angles randomly. Cut only either the threads of the weft, or the warp threads

is almost impossible. As a result of the foregoing, and when examining the edges of all the damages on the tent, one can conclude that three damages /conditionally marked № 1, 2, 3 / came as a result of contact with some sharp weapon /knife/, i.e. are cuts. Yet the rest of the damage is a tear. Damage # 1 is shaped in the form of a broken straight line, its total length is 32 cm. Above it there is a small puncture of the tissue in 2 cm. The corners of the hole are torn. Damage # 2 and 3 have a non-uniform arcuate shape. The approximate length of these lesions is 89 cm and 42 cm. from the right edge of damage # 2 and from both edges of damage # 3 there are no cloth flaps and it is possible that they had their continuation further. In order to determine from which side the indicated cuts were made (from the inner one - from the tent or from the outside), a thorough microscopic examination of the edges of the cuts of the adjacent tissue sections was made / zoom level from 0.6 to 56X /. As a result of the conducted studies it was found that from the inside of the tent in the areas of the cuts close to the edges there are surface damages of the fabric in the form of minor punctures, incisions of the fabric threads and very thin scratches. All scratches and punctures are rectilinear. Scratches are observed in the surface damage of the filaments: the filaments are either cut in half / see photo № 10 /, or with them the dye is simply scratched off and not the colored parts are visible. At the corners of the punctures, on the inside of the tent / unlike the outer tent, there are, as it were, continuations of damage, which are expressed in the form of thin scratches. The nature and shape of all these injuries indicate that they were formed from the contact of the fabric of the inner side of the tent with the blade of some weapon /knife/. All of the above indicates that the existing incisions are made from the inside, from the tent.

CONCLUSION

In the camping tent of Dyatlov group on the right slant of the canopy forming the roof, three damages of approximately 32, 89, and 42 cm in length /conditionally numbered 1, 2, 3 / are made with some sharp weapon /knife/ i.e. are cuts.

All these cuts are done on the inside of the tent.

Seal   EXPERT

SR. RESEARCH ASSOCIATE Churkina - signature
/CHURKINA/

Part VII

1

Endings

The investigation did not establish the presence of other people on February 1 or February 2, 1959 in the area of the height "1079", except the tourists from Dyatlov group. It is also established that the population of the Mansi people, living in 80-100 km from this place, is Russian friendly, offers tourists accommodation, assistance etc. The place where the group died is considered to be unfit for hunting and reindeer breeding in the winter.

Considering the absence of external injuries to the bodies or signs of a fight, the presence of all the valuables of the group, and also taking into account the conclusion of the medical examinations for the causes of the deaths of the tourists, it is concluded that the cause of their demise was an overwhelming force, which the tourists were not able to overcome.

For the shortcomings in the organization of tourist work and weak control of the Bureau of the Sverdlovsk GC the CPSU punished in party terms: the director of the Ural Polytechnic Institute Siunov, the secretary of the party bureau Zaostrovsky, the chairman of the trade union UPK Slobodin, the chairman of the city union of voluntary sports societies Kurochkin and the inspector of the union Ufimtsev. The chairman of the board of the sports club of the Gordo Institute has been removed from work.

Given that between the actions of the above-mentioned persons who have committed shortcomings in the formulation of sports work and the death of tourists, there is no causal connection and, not seeing in this case the corpus delicti, *guided by paragraph 5 of Article 4 of the RSFSR Code of Criminal Procedure,*

r u l e d :

The criminal case on the death of the group of tourists and further proceedings are to be terminated.

> *PROSECUTOR CRIMINALIST*
> *JR. ADVISER OF JUSTICE (IVANOV)*
> *AGREED:*
> *DEPUTY CHIEF OF THE INVESTIGATIVE DEPARTMENT*
> *ADVISER OF JUSTICE (LUKIN)*

Theorists cite that closing the case was suspicious as if there were a cover-up. The route was closed to hikers for several year. If anything, the government was embarrassed that nine young people had died. The university provided little as far as supplies and money, and the tourists were not well-equipped. It was something the government didn't want repeated.

There was no sign of criminal action, so the case was closed. An "overwhelming force" implies nature.

The preparation of the members of the group to participate in a difficult winter hike in the mountains was clearly insufficient. The focus was on skiing, general equipment, products.

According to the plan of the expedition, they had to go through five passes and climb two peaks, but they did not have any safety equipment (ropes, strapping, carabiners, rappel gear), or any other climbing equipment (ice axes, crampons).

In the training materials, only a 20-meter-long prusik is mentioned (a thin auxiliary rope not suitable for securing), which was not found during inspections. There was only one ice ax found at the tent and, according to the photos, belonged to A.A. Zolotaryov.

Meanwhile, in the winter, the Northern Urals are characterized by strong (to −50 °) frosts and storm winds. Therefore, almost all passes and peaks have extensive ice and icy slopes of compacted snow (firn), which is very difficult to traverse without special skills and equipment.

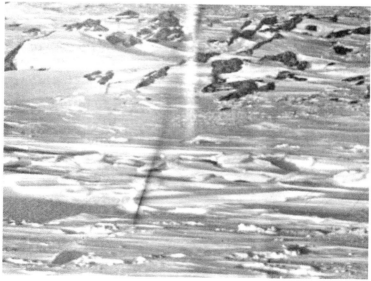

2

I was critical of the investigation, but Shkryabach Sergey Yakovlevich,veteran investigative and forensic services, stated his problems with the investigation far more clearly:

"A tent on the slope was discovered and dug out of snow on February 26, 1959 by B.E. Slobtsov group (a mountaineer with little experience at the time of the events). The site was examined by the prosecutor of Ivdel only on February 28, 1959, after significant changes in the situation.

The body of R.V. Slobodin (found on March 5, 1959) and the place of its discovery were not examined at all.

The bodies of L.A. Dubinina, A.S. Kolevatov, A.A. Zolotaryov and N.V. Thibeaux-Brignolle were found on May 4, 1959 and examined on the spot on May 6, 1959. At the same time the items found with the bodies are not mentioned in the protocol at all.

As already noted, the measurement data on the location of the tent and the bodies indicated in the inspection reports do not correspond to the data set out in the materials of the aforementioned commission and in the decision to terminate the criminal case.

There is no information about attempts to analyze weather conditions for the estimated period of death of the group and their changes until the moment of the search works in the criminal case or in the materials of the commission. Meanwhile, the commission's conclusion shows that if at the beginning of the search expedition the weather conditions were acceptable, by the end of February - the beginning of March the weather deteriorated sharply, the frost increased, and the blizzards and hurricane winds began, despite the fact that the bodies of four tourists were still missing, and served as the basis for the termination of the search on March 8, 1959.

There is no data on studies of the snow-ice cover in the area of the tragedy to determine the characteristics of its layers, stages and conditions for their formation. With this in mind, no attempts were made to invite relevant specialists (meteorologists, seismologists, glaciologists, psychologists, climbers, etc.) to conduct case studies on the mechanism and sequence of the situation and the actions of the group members with the collection, analysis and evaluation of objective data.

The investigation did not even make an attempt to independently model the event mechanism, compare and analyze the position and condition of the tent at the time of its detection (and not at the time of inspection), traces around it to determine how could they leave, the sequence and direction of movement of the group, taking into account the characteristics of the terrain and wind. Instead was taken into account the opinion of the often unseasoned tourists about the safety of the camp setup in such conditions and the allegedly sufficient experience among the hikers.

As a result of the amateurish assessment of this situation, the true causes and conditions for the emergency evacuation from the tent were not established, and a whole "bunch" of shady (not mentioned in the criminal case) versions of the existence of some unknown forces and secret events made the victims flee the tent in a panic, condemning themselves to death in conditions of snowstorms, hurricane winds and 40 degrees of cold. This led to the appearance of information in the case of fireballs, radiological studies of the clothing of victims, etc., which, of course, did not provide anything for the investigation. (...)

The fact that they, in severe frost, half-clothed, left the tent on their own and six of them froze, and three died, including from serious injuries of internal organs, is no reason to relate everything that happened to the action of overwhelming force without studying and explaining the causes, circumstances and mechanism of these events.(...)

Landmarks and detailed photographs were not taken during the inspections of the incident sites. Available photos can be called survey only conditionally. Accurate measurements and reference to specific landmarks of detected objects and bodies are not available in the protocols. Plans (schemes) were not drawn up by prosecutors and investigators. It is almost impossible to establish from the investigation materials exactly where the tent and the bodies were found. (...)

Based on the above, the circumstances of the deaths of tourists have no hidden motive, and all the questions and doubts that have arisen are the consequences of lack of professionalism and incomplete work on the case. However, to fill the gaps in the investigation, taking into account past years, there are currently only limited possibilities. It seems that given the lack of objective data on the involvement of anyone in the death of members."

3

In many ways, the expedition was set up to fail, but it didn't have to fail.

While all of the hikers/skiers had experience, the tourists didn't have enough experience for the conditions that they faced. Being prepared for a severe storm, hypoxia, and exhaustion wasn't natural; it was impossible to prepare for the unknown. Mountaineers must handle those situations as they happen, and luckily a combination of serious factors don't occur often. While I applaud Igor as a leader and the others for their abilities, they were just not ready for everything to go wrong at once.

The lack of proper supplies is appalling. When I first began my research into the case, I was immediately shocked at the fact that there were no carabiners or ropes. In an emergency, such as that of Semyon's fall, there was nothing to safely help him out of the ravine. There was nothing to properly build a sledge to carry anyone out of the area. There was no way to communicate and no contingency plans.

Waiting two weeks and expecting a search and *rescue* was beyond imagination. Officials should have been notified far sooner.

The investigation was not perfect, but the situation was to blame; the scene was enormous, searchers wanted to find the missing tourists above all, and no one was properly prepared to investigate the case. The missing or ruined evidence is lost forever, but I don't believe the problems were intentional.

On the evening of February 1, 1959, besides the snow storm, a secondary storm struck, terrifying the group. They already had the first stages of hypoxia, so confusion, anxiety, fear, and disorientation were magnified. Once on the slope, they attempted to warm themselves, but it was far too late. There was probably an arctic vortex as well. Falls into the ravine concluded the tragedy. Because of many factors, but above all, because of nature, the group never stood a chance.

I understand the obsession with this case. It's mysterious, heart-breaking, somewhat unsolved, and has a terrible lack of substantiated evidence. Or evidence at all.

When I began this, I had trouble with names and who was who and who did what. Then everything changed. Somehow, I began to get to know the tourists through photographs, interviews, the letters their parents wrote after the event, and their diaries. They became people that I knew and who had died and left behind many questions about their deaths. That was when my obsession began.

Regardless of what explanation I found, it was secondary. The Dyatlov Nine mattered. Period.

I admire Igor for his leadership abilities and adore his open, unself-conscious smile; I would have been one of his friends. He was brilliant with inventions, and the world will never know what he might have done to revolutionize radios.

Lyuda had a beautiful, innocent outlook and had so much to look forward to. I respect that as young as she was, she was fierce and strong. She was cautious but kind to others.

There is no doubt that Zina would have made a spectacular mother because of her chemistry with children. I am in awe of how much love and goodness she held in her heart.

Sasha was smart, mature, and goal-driven; I wish I had even a tenth of his focus. He would have been someone great one day. He was such a good father-figure that there is no doubt he would have made an excellent father to children of his own.

Kolya (Nicolai) was smart, very handsome, kind, funny, driven to succeed, and the sort of man that most young women dream of marrying. He had it all; plus, he never gave up on a goal. Everyone loved him.

NICOLAI.

YURI.

Yuri was a romantic, exceptionally brave, and I admire that he was unselfish. When he left the tent, he knew he was condemned to suffer in the weather, yet he didn't complain. He grew up poor but was working hard to better himself; that's impressive.

Rustik is one whom I never got to know as well, but I do know he was courageous, goal oriented, intelligent, and I stand by my assertation that he was also unselfish and caring.

Semyon. I don't know if I portrayed him as trying to be a hero in getting the rest out of the tent or as a villain who caused their deaths, but I intended the former. I believe he did everything he could to save the tourists when they were at the cedar tree. Same for the ravine. I think that at the time, when at the tent, he did what his brain said to do, and it made sense at the time and in the situation. I suspect that he was somewhat tortured by what he saw during the war on the front lines. He was brave enough to win four medals. From the photos, I know he had a good sense of humor, and from diaries, I know that the others in the group grew to like him. I ended up liking him greatly.

Georgy is my Achilles heel. For some reason, although I can't describe him beyond being funny, sweet, smart, tough, hard-working, and brave, there is something more that alludes me. I felt connected to him almost from the beginning, and when I had to write about his death, I was sad. He somehow has had the ability to reach beyond death and allow me to get to know him the best; giving me inspiration.

For some, the story itself draws me in, but the Dyatlov Nine keep me interested and, in cases, obsessed. Some need answers because as bad as events were on February 1, people want to find something that makes it all not quite so random and useless. They need a meaning for tourists' deaths.

Maybe that meaning is for better standards in mountaineering. Or in faster rescue responses. Maybe some have learned better investigative techniques.

There is no answer.

Sometimes, no meanings can be found in a tragedy. In those cases, the only way to move on is to remember those who are lost, in this case, Igor, Zina, Lyuda, Sasha, Koyla, Rustik, Semyon, Yuri, and Georgy. The Dyatlov Nine.

Texarkana, Tx
February 2019

Part VIII

I wish to thank the following:

The people who contributed to the case files: witnesses, experts, investigators, searchers, and Yuri Yudin, the only survivor of the original group. The Russian government for allowing the use of the case files.

Nick for his help teaching me about Russian culture and language, taking photographs, and for telling me about the case. He also went over every detail of the case to keep me sharp and bought me my beloved Orlov jersey.

DA Roberts for his invaluable help with crime scenes and for brainstorming ideas at 3:00 AM. I appreciate that he used the autopsy materials to form stronger arguments.

Brad Hammock for helping me understand the psychology of mountaineers and the many variables involved with the sport, for discussing theories, and for causing me to think outside the box.

My Russian hockey players Orlov and Ovechkin who spiked my love of their culture.

David, for making me laugh at his funny theories when I was getting far too intense. He also explained a lot about the psychology of former military.

Vyv Pratt who took on a huge task. I asked her to ignore the case and anything written and to look at the pictures and give me sketches based of what she saw within each person's eyes. I needed her to show me psychology based on photographs alone which is a two-part process. She provided me exactly what I needed: I saw each person how I wished to. Alive and strong.

To the Dyatlov Nine. Rest in peace.

Part IX

Autopsy Reports and Photographs

*Over 18 only.
*Viewer discretion: reports and photos are extremely graphic.

*** Note that these are the original reports and grammar, spelling, and content have NOT been altered.

MEDICAL-FORENSIC EXAMINATION OF SLOBODIN Rustem Vladimirovich, 23

External examination:
On the examination table is a male body posed as follows: the head of the body is angled backwards with the chin forwards and pointing upwards, the right arm in the right shoulder joint is slightly angled and bent at a right angle at the elbow. The fingers are clenched into a fist. The left arm is drawn back and to the side and is straight at the elbow. On the arm is a Zvezda-brand watch showing the time 8 hours 45 minutes. The right leg is bent at the pelvis at an angle of 120 degrees and at the knee at a right angle. The left leg is bent at the pelvis at a right angle and at the knee at an angle of 60 degrees. Both legs are touching each other in the area of the internal surface of the lower area of the thigh and the upper third of the shin.

The body is clothed as follows: a black cotton sweater. Under this is a checked shirt with black and red squares buttoned with three buttons and the cuffs each buttoned with two buttons. The checked shirt has a left pocket fastened with a safety pin. In the pocket is a passport with the name SLOBODIN Rustem Vladimirovich, 310 rubles (one 100 note, four 50 notes and 10 rubles) and a fountain pen with ink. In between the checked shirt and the sweater are two insoles from boots. Under the checked shirt is a warm undershirt and a fleece sweatshirt fastened with two buttons. Under this is a blue knitted shirt with long arms. Warm ski pants fasted with a button and a belt. In the pockets are a pack of matches with 48 matches, a pocket knife on a long string, a comb in a case, two pieces of string and a pencil, and a cotton sock. Under these are satin sports pants, in the back pocket of which is a letter from the trade union committee dated 20 January 1959. Under the sports pants are warm, grey, fleece long underwear fully buttoned/pair from shirt. Under the long underwear are blue satin underpants with elastic. On the right leg is a black felt boot. Under the boot are cotton socks, and then grey woolen socks, a cotton sock, and a brown vigogne sock. The felt boot is missing from the left leg, but there are socks in the same order as the other leg. On the head there is dark blond curly hair with a length of up to 8 cm. The forehead is high and slanting towards the back. The skin of the face is blue-red in color.

Postmortem lividity is present with blue-red spots abundantly located on the rear surface of the neck, torso and limbs. Rigor mortis has resolved in the muscle groups of the joints. In the area of the centre of the forehead there are small abrasions that are brown-red in color with parchment density and slightly indented. Above them are two scoring marks that are linear in shape under dry brown crust with a length of up to 1.5 cm located parallel to and about 0.3 cm from each other. The eyebrows are blond and bushy. The eyes are partially open. On the upper right eyelid there is an abrasion that is brown-red in color with a size of 1 x 0.5 cm. In the area of the abrasion and scoring marks on the face there is hemorrhaging into the underlying soft tissue. The cornea is cloudy, the iris is grayish brown in color, and the pupils are dilated. There are Lyarshe spots on the cornea. The bridge of the nose is straight. The soft tissue on the bridge and the top of the nose is brown-red in color. On the end of the nose a part of the soft tissue is under a dry brown-cherry-red crust with a size of 1.5 x 1 cm. The lips are swollen. The mouth is closed. There is a trail of caked blood coming from the opening of the nose. The rims of the lips are brown-cherry-red in color and are dry and wrinkled. The teeth are even and white. The tongue is whole and behind the teeth. The mucosa of the tongue and gums is pale grey in color.

The right side of the face is slightly swollen. Underneath it are many small abrasions of uneven form and parchment density under a dry crust partially extending to the area of the chin. On the left side of the face are abrasions of the same character; one of them is an abrasion that is 1.2 x 0.4 cm in size under a dry brown crust in the area of the left malar mound. The ears are ovular in form and reddish blue in color. On the outer edge of the right ear the soft tissue is brown-cherry-red in color, solid when palpated, and of parchment density. The left ear is the same. The openings of the mouth and ears are clean. On the left side of the neck there are dark red abrasions. The chest is cylindrically shaped. The stomach is located at the level of the chest. The skin of the torso and the upper limbs down to the wrist joints, as well as the lower limbs, are of [blue?] pink color. The soft tissue of the surface of the back and palms of the hands are brown-purple in color. In the area of the wrist joint of the hand there is a graze wound protruding from the soft tissue in an area 8 x 1.5 cm in size covered in dry parchment-density crust under the layer of skin. Along the edge of the ulnar of the left hand there is a graze wound of brown cherry-red color and parchment density 6 x 2 cm in size with the transferring of the graze wound to the lateral surface of the left hand. In the area of the terminal phalanx of both hands the soft tissue is shriveled and solid when palpated. On the lower third of the rear side of the right forearm there are two parts of the epidermis that are missing with sizes of 2.5 x 3 cm and 3.5 x 1.5 cm with uneven edges and pale red color. On the front inner surface of the upper limbs. The venous system is well-pronounced. The external genitals are properly formed. The head of the penis is pink-red in color, shriveled, and solid when palpated. The opening of the anus is clear. The venous system is well-pronounced on the feet. There is 'bath skin' on the feet. There are graze wounds in the soft tissue of the lower left shin that are dark red in color and 2.5 x 1.5 and 4.5 x 1.5 in size.

The skin flaps of the skull are moist, juicy and shiny. In the corresponding right lobular area and left and right lobular muscles there is a spilling hemorrhage into the soft tissue. There is a bone fracture from the left temporal bone along the direction of the upper forward area of the lobular bone with dehiscence of 0.1 cm and a length of up to 6 cm. The fracture is 1.5 cm from the sagittal suture. In addition to this, there is a discrepancy in the joint temporal-parietal suture on the left and right /post-mortem/. The dura mater is bluish in color, and its vessels are slightly filled with blood. There was 75 cm3 of bloody liquid under the dura mater. The pia is cloudy and red green in color. The brain matter appears as an unformed mass that is green red in color with undifferentiated contours of the ventricles, as well as the white and grey matter. In the upper area of the left pyramid there is hemorrhaging under the left bone plate with a size of 0.3 x 0.4 cm. The bones of the skull base are whole.The subcutaneous fat of the body is decently developed. The internal organs are properly located. The pleural cavity contained up to one litre of bloody liquid /effusion/. The pericardial sac contained 30 cm3 of bloody liquid. The size of the heart is 11 x 10 x 6 cm. When sectioned, the heart muscle is dark red in color; the thickness of the muscle of the left ventricle is 1.5 cm, and the right is 0.5 cm. The right and left parts of the heart contained up to 100 cm3 of dark liquid blood. The valves of the heart, aorta and pulmonary arteries are smooth, thin and cloudy dark red color. The coronary vessels of the heart are freely passable. The internal surface of the aorta is smooth and clean. The surface of the lungs is blue-red in color and dough-like when palpated. When sectioned the lung tissue is dark red in color. When pressed, a large amount of foamy bloody liquid and dark liquid blood is released from the surface. The lumen of the larynx and bronchi are free. The mucosa of the esophagus, trachea and bronchi are pink-red in color. The stomach contained about 100 cm3 of a brown-yellow mucous mass. The mucosa of the stomach is turgid and grey-red in color with the good expression of the folds. There are Vishnevsky spot hemorrhages on the surface of the folds of the stomach. The horns of the sublingual bone are whole. When sectioned, the thyroid is red in color. When sectioned, the pancreas is pinkish-red in color. The surface of the liver is smooth and bright. The liver is 23 x 16 x 12 x 7 cm in size. When sectioned the liver tissue is brown-cherry-red in color, very filled with blood, and with poor differentiation of the hepatic pattern. The gall bladder contained up to 30 (or 80? Approximated) cm3 of brown liquid; its mucosa is velvety and of brown-yellow color. The mucosa is flabby when palpated. When sectioned the tissue is dark-cherry-red in color. The pulp is removed from the section under heavy scraping. The size of the mucosa is 11 x 7 x 3 cm.

The lumen of the small intestine contained a mucus mass of dirty yellow color. The lumen of the large intestine contained a partially formed fecal mass. The mucosa of the stomach is blue-grey in color. The surface of the kidneys is smooth and bright. The size of the right kidney is 11 x 5 x 3 cm, and the left is 10 x 5 x 3 cm. When sectioned the kidney tissue is dark cherry red in color. The cortex and medulla layers are well differentiated. The layers of the adrenal gland are well differentiated. In the area of the right adrenal there is hemorrhage into the brain matter. The bladder contained up to 200 cm3 of cloudy pale-yellow liquid. The mucosa of the bladder is bluish. For chemical and histological analysis, parts of the internal organs and part of the pyramid of the temporal bone were removed.

During the investigation, traces of alcohol were not detected.

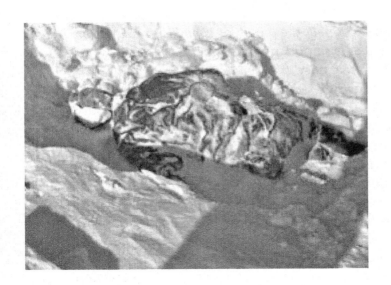

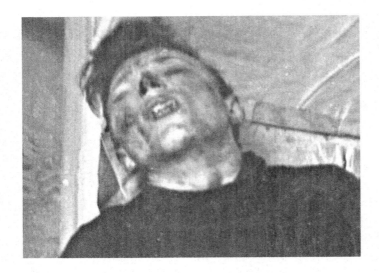

"Based on the data of the examination of the body of Slobodin Rustem Vladimirovich, 23 years old, and considering the circumstances of the case, I believe that the death of Slobodin was caused by the action of low temperature/freezing, which is evidenced by the swelling of the meninges, the blood-filled internal organs, the Vishnevksy spots on the stomach mucosa, and the third- and fourth-degree freezing of the fingers. The fracture of the left frontal lobe bone could have occurred during a fall by Slobodin or the impact of the head on a hard object such as rocks, ice, etc. A blunt object caused the above-mentioned trauma. When this happened, it would have caused Slobodin to become stunned and allowed for his rapid freezing. The absence of explicit bleeding under the meninges allows for the assumption that Slobodin's death came as a result of his freezing. The injuries found on Slobodin's body in the form of abrasions, scrapes and graze wounds were caused by a blunt object as the result of a fall or injury on rocks, ice, etc.

The damage was caused during life, as well as in the agonal state and post mortem.

The data of the examination of Slobodin's body allows for the presumption that his last meal was 6-8 hours before the time of death. The presence of alcohol was not detected during the examination. Taking account these injuries, in the first hour after they happened Slobodin was able to move and crawl. Slobodin's death was violent and accidental."

MEDICAL-FORENSIC EXAMINATION OF DOROSHENKO
Yuri Alekseevich, 21

external examination:

The body under examination is a male body of regular build. The body position is as follows: the upper limbs are drawn up at the shoulder joints towards the head and are bent at the elbow joints. The finger joints are also bent. The lower limbs are stretched. The head is turned to the left.

The body was found with the following clothes on it: a short-sleeved blue and red checked shirt with two two-button patch pockets and with all six buttons buttoned up, a sleeveless light-green knitted vest, blue sateen pants and briefs, and blue knitted long underwear with two buttons buttoned up. In the middle third of the thigh, on the inner thigh to the left and on the front thigh to the right the long underwear is torn: there is a 22 x 23 cm fabric tear on the right and another 13 x 13 cm fabric tear on the left. On the left foot, there are two pairs of light-brown knitted socks torn in the back of the foot and in the ankle joint and a white woolen sock with a reinforced heel; on a white sock there is a 2 x 5 cm dark-brown burnt area in the forefoot around the toe. On the right foot, there are the remains of the cotton sock with an elastic band. This sock is the same color as the one on the left foot. There is also a white woolen sock. On the inside of the pants, there is an identification tag reading 5П1513.

The length of the body is 180 cm. The body has a good nutritional status and well-developed muscle groups. Crimson purple post-mortem stains are located on the back of the neck, torso and limbs. Rigor mortis has resolved in the muscle groups of the joints. There is dark 6-cm-long chestnut hair on the head, cut in a crew-cut style. In the temporoparietal and occipital zones, there is an area where the ends of the hair are burnt. The hair is dirty with moss remains and fir needles. The skin of the face is brown-purple. The contour of the face is smoothed. The eyebrows are dark chestnut and thick. The eyes are closed, the corneas are cloudy, the irises are brown, the pupils are enlarged, and the eyelid mucosa is pale pink. The nasal ridge is straight. Around the nasal ridge, the nasal tip and the upper lip, there are clotted blood traces. The upper lip is swollen. Around the vermilion border of the upper lip, there is a 1.5 x 2 cm dark red hemorrhage. The mouth is slightly opened. The teeth are white and even. The mucous membrane of the gums and the vestibule of the mouth is pale red. The tongue is in the oral cavity behind the teeth. Around the right cheek, the soft tissue is covered with a layer of foamy grey fluid. Grey fluid traces are also visible around the opening of the mouth. The auricles are oval in shape and bluish red in color. Around the tragus and the lobule of the right auricle, there is a 6 x 1.5 cm thick brown red area. On the left auricle around the tragus, there is a similar 4 x 1 cm brown red parchmentlike area. The auricles are bright red from the inside. (illegible) without any distinctive features. On the inner arms and forearms of both upper limbs, the venous pattern is well-defined. Soft tissues of the upper limbs are bluish red.

On the inner right arm, in the middle third, there are two 2 x 1.5 cm irregular-shaped brown red parchment-like abrasions without hemorrhages in the adjacent tissue. In the area of these abrasions, two linear incisions are made. By the anterior margin of the right axillary line, there is a 2 x 1.5 cm dark red skin abrasion area. On the front of the right arm, there are small brown red scab-like abrasions without hemorrhages in the adjacent tissues. In the upper third of the right forearm, there are 4 (?) x 1-, 2.5 x 1.5 and 5 x 0.5 cm stripe-shaped brown red abrasions. There are also small abrasions in the lower third of the right forearm. On the back (illegible) of the right hand, there is swelling of the soft tissue and small abrasions. On the back of the hand, specifically on the second metacarpal bone, there is a 2 x 1.5 cm brown-red abrasion with hemorrhaging into the adjacent tissue. The soft tissue of the hand and fingers, especially the distal phalanges, are dark purple. On the inner left arm, in the lower third, there are 3 x 0.5, 1.5 x 0.7 and 1 x 1.5 cm brown red abrasions. On the sides of the left elbow joint, there are small brown-red grazes as well as 2 x 3 cm abrasions of the same color with the parallel stripe-shaped sliding traces. On the inner left forearm, between the middle third and the lower third, there is a 0.6 x 0.5 cm irregular-shaped oval skin wound. The edges of the wound are slightly pressed down and covered with clotted blood. An incision was made around this wound and hemorrhaging in the adjacent soft tissues was found. The soft tissue in the back of the left hand is slightly swollen and brown-red in color. The distal phalanges of the fingers are dark purple. The thoracic cage is cylindrical in shape. The abdomen is located slightly lower than the thoracic cage. In the iliac area, there is an 8 cm linear whitish scar. The external genital organs are properly formed. In the area of the glans penis and foreskin, the soft tissue is bright red. The openings of the anus and urethra are clean. The muscle groups of the lower limbs are well-developed. On the back and inner thighs and shins, the venous pattern is well-defined. On the front shins, in the middle third, there are pale red parchment-like abrasions – 8 x 4 cm on the left shin and 5 x 1.5 cm on the right shin. The soft tissue in the distal phalanges of the toes is dark purple. Examination by touch shows that the skeleton bones and cartilages are intact.

Internal examination

The skin flaps of the scalp are moist, rich, glossy, and pale red from the inside. The skullcap and skull base bones are intact. The dura mater is bluish and hyperaemic. The pia mater is opaque and swollen. Convolutions and fissures of the brain are smoothed out and flattened. The brain matter is a greenish red jelly-like substance. The grey matter can hardly be distinguished from the white matter. Brain ventricle contours are indistinguishable. The cerebellum matter pattern is poorly distinguished. The base of the brain vessels is regular. The subcutaneous fat of the body is well-developed. The position of the internal organs is normal. The pleural cavities are empty. The pericardium contained about 40 cm3 of amber fluid. The size of the heart is 13 x10 x 6 cm. The cardiac muscle is dark red when sectioned. The left ventricle muscle is 2 cm thick, while the right ventricle muscle is 0.7 cm thick, in the right and left half of the heart was contained up to 270 cm3. liquid dark blood, the hearts of the aorta and pulmonary artery are smooth, thin, shiny, pale red; the coronary arteries are free, the arteries are enlarged, we pass well; inside the aortic surface smooth, clean, the width of the aortic arch ?? valves 8.5 cm. The lungs from the surface bluish red ??? color, testovaty to the touch, on the sections of the lung tissue of dark color, when pressed from the surface of the cut st. in a large quantity of liquid dark blood and foamy liquid; the larynx and bronchus lumen is free; mucous esophagus, trachea, bronchus bluish-red color. ???? the sub-lingual bone is intact. Thyroid gland on the incision of a flock of reddish color. The ventricle contained about 150 cm3 liquid mucous mass of reddish color, the mucous membrane of the stomach is lilac red, swollen, with well-expressed folding; On the upper surface of the folds of the stomach there is a large number of small hemorrhages - spots of Vishnevsky. A sour smell is felt by the sense of smell from the contents of the stomach. The pancreas is in section small-lobed lilac-red. In the lumen of the small intestine contained a mucus mass of reddish color, the mucosa of the intestine of a bluish-red color. In the large intestine, semi formed feces are light-brown in color, the mucosa of the intestine is pale-gray. The spleen is flabby to the touch, the capsule is wrinkled, the size of the spleen is 1 x 7 x 3 cm, the tissue of its dark-cherry color on the incisions, the pulp gives a slight scraping from the surface of the incision. The liver from the surface is smooth, shiny, the liver is 9 x 12 x 10 cm in size, the liver tissue is brownish, full-blooded, the liver tissue is poorly visible, the gall bladder contains up to 30 cm. 3. Olfactory fluid, buccal velvety buccal mucosa colors. The kidneys from the surface are smooth, shiny, the capsule is easily removed from them, the size of the right kidney is 11 x 6 x 4 cm, the left kidney is 11 x 5 x 3.5 cm, the tissue of the buds is dark-cherry on the cut, the layers of the kidneys are poorly discernible. The layers of the adrenal glands are clearly distinguishable. The bladder contained about 150 cm 3 of a cloudy, light yellow liquid; the mucosa of the bladder is pale of the color. In the study of internal organs, the presence of alcohol was not detected.

Some organs from the body under examination have been taken for chemical and histological testing to the Regional Laboratory.

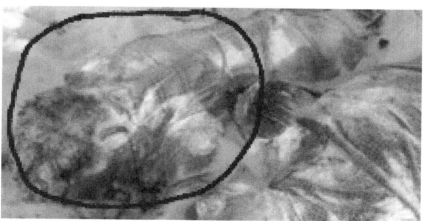

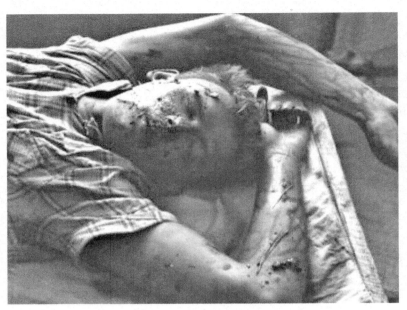

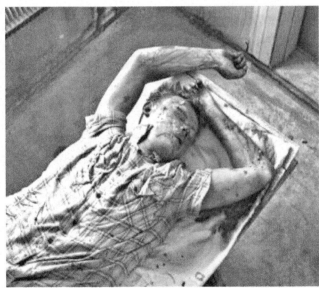

"According to the examination results of the body belonging to Doroshenko Yuri Nikolayevich, aged 21, and considering the circumstances of the case, we believe that the death occurred as the result of low temperature exposure (freezing), which can be proved by the following evidence: meninges oedema, strong hyperaemia in the internal organs, cardiac cavities full of liquid dark blood, petechiae in the gastric mucosa (known as Vishnevsky spots), an excessively full bladder, along with the third and fourth degree frostbite of fingers and toes.

External examination showed damage, such as multiple abrasions and skin wounds caused by a blunt object that could occur as the result of falling or bruising against stones, ice, and other objects. The injuries mentioned above occurred while alive, during the agonal state, and after death. The injuries mentioned above can be described as slight injuries without damage to health. This examination of the body gives reasons to state that the last meal was consumed 6 to 8 hours before death. Alcohol was not found during the tests. The death is violent and accidental."

MEDICAL-FORENSIC EXAMINATION OF KRIVONISCHENKO Georgiy Alekseevich, 23

external examination

On the examination table is a male body. The pose of the body is as follows: the head is turned to the left, the right arm is bent upwards at the elbow, the fingers of the right hand are touching the head, the left arm is bent at the elbow and is equilibrated with the shoulder, the hand is bent and the fingers are touching the chest. The right leg is straight, and the left leg is slightly diverted at the hip and bent at the knee.

The body is clothed as follows: a blue cotton checked shirt with red and black squares and three buttons, two of which are unbuttoned, with the cuffs fastened with two buttons. In the outside pocket is a coil of copper wire and a pink silk ribbon. To the left on the inside surface a pocket from white material has been sewn in. Under the checked shirt is a white cotton undershirt and white long underwear made from 'Gribzon' material. The bottom left half of the long underwear is missing up to the knee; the edge of the tear is uneven and charred. Under the long underwear are blue satin shorts on 2 (illegible). On the left leg is a torn cotton sock, the edges of which are burned.

The male body is 169 cm long, of proper constitution, good nutrition and well-developed muscle groups of the torso and limbs. Postmortem lividity is present in purple spots located on the back surface of the neck, torso and limbs. Rigor mortis has resolved in the muscle groups of the joints. On the head is butch-cut dark blond curly hair with a length of up to 10 cm. The forehead is high and slanting to the back. The eyebrows are dark blond and thick. The skin of the face is blue-grey in color. In the middle part of the brow there is a round contusion with a size of 0.3 x 0.3 cm brown-red color and with parchment density. In the left temporal area are two abrasions grazes of brown-red color with sizes of 1.2 x?.3 cm and 1 x 0.2 cm. The eyes are half open. The right eye fissure is larger than the left. The corneas of the right and left eyes have Lyarshe spots. The corneas are cloudy, the iris is grey-green in color, the pupils are dilated, and the mucous membrane is pale grey in color. The nasal dorsum is straight. In the middle third of the nose there is a graze wound of brown-red color and crusting, turning into a wound at the end of the nose and wings with a defect in the soft tissue of a size of 1.8 x 2 cm; the nasal septum cartilage appears at the bottom of the wound and to the right is the nasal passage. On the lower [the first part of the word is not recognizable, approximate state] lip and chin is ash-colored hair with a length of up to 0.5 cm. The mucous membrane of the lip is dark brown in color with crusted epidermis. The mouth is shut, and the lips are swollen. Behind the bottom periodontal flaps, the epidermis is pale grey in color with papillary lines on the flaps with a size of 1.8 x 0.6 cm. The teeth are straight with white enamel. The opening of the mouth and nose are clear. On the cheeks there are dark brown abrasions with stiffened epidermis and contusions of the same color. The external ears are swollen and blue-red in color. The neck is normal. The chest is cylindrical. The external genitals are properly formed. The opening of the anus is clean. The skin of the chest, neck and limbs down to the wrists is reddish purple in color with the showing of the venous system on the limbs. There are pale-red abrasions measuring 7 x 2 cm on the right side of the chest on the level of the armpit without hemorrhaging into the underlying tissue. In the costal margin of the right hypochondrium along the clavicle line there are pale-red abrasions of parchment density with sizes of 2 x 1.2 cm and 1 x 1.2 cm without hemorrhaging into the underlying tissue. The rear of the right hand is swollen. In the area of the metacarpophalangeal joints the soft tissue is whitish grey in color. The fingers are brown-purple in color. The terminal phalanx is dry and dark brown in color. On the rear of these fingers are small dark brown skin abrasions of parchment density. The surface of the palm of the right hand is blue-red in color and there are skin wounds with uneven borders that are dark red in color at the rear of the thumb. On the middle phalanx of the third [changed from the word 'middle'] finger is a defect in the epidermis with the same shape and form as that found in the oral cavity.

The terminal phalanx of all fingers of dark brown color. In the area of the radiocarpal joint is a dark red graze wound crusted over with a size of 5 x 2.5 cm. The rear area of the left hand is swollen. There is a scalpel wound across the whole cross-section of the left hand with exfoliated epidermis of dark brown color and parchment density with a size of 8 x 2 cm. The rear area of fingers 2-5 on the left hand are black in color with the shriveling of the epidermis of finger 5 and dried-up terminal phalanxes. There are dark brown flesh wounds on the middle phalanx of fingers 4-5 with sizes of 1.5 x 1 cm and 1 x 0.5 cm that are solid when palpated and are charred. On the surface of the left buttocks and thigh, parts of the soft tissue are pink and brown-red in color with parchment density with the drooping of the epidermis at parts with sizes of 10 x 3 cm, 6 x 2 cm, and 4 x 5 cm. On the anterior surface of the inner thigh there are graze wounds that are dark brown and dark red in color with parchment density and sizes of (illegible) x 2, 1 x 1.5 cm and smaller. On the internal surface of the thigh there are three flesh wounds of (illegible) form with even edges and a depth of 0.3 cm with sharp angles with a size of 1.5 x 0.4 cm. The left shin and ?? are swollen. There is a burn across the entire surface of the left anticnemion with a size of 31 x 10 cm with parchment density. In the lower third of the left (illegible) of brown-black color with charred tissue and the blow out of the cutaneous covering (illegible) in the middle and upper thirds there is an ambustial surface (illegible)red and light brown color. On the rear inside surface of the left shin there is an abrasion of dark brown color with parchment density and sizes of 8 x 1.3 cm, (illegible) x 1.5 cm, and 2 x 1 cm. The rear of the left foot is dark brown in color with subcutaneous defects of the epidermis with a size of 10 x 4 cm. (illegible) of the second toe is charred and the skin is dark brown in color ??? solid when palpated. On the front surface of the right thigh and shin there are dark brown abrasions with parchment density measuring 5 x 2 cm, 3 x 8 cm, 7 x 1 cm and 2 x (illegible) cm.

Internal examination

The interior surface of the skin flaps of the scalp is moist, shiny and red in color. In the right ?? area and occipital region there is diffuse hemorrhaging seeping into the right temporal muscle. The bones of the base of the skull are intact. The dura mater is blue-?? and full of blood. The pia is muddy and swollen. The gyrus and sulcus are poorly distinguished. The brain matter has a jelly-like appearance and is reddish green in color. The grey matter is poorly distinguished from the white. The contours of the lateral ventricles of the brain are poorly distinguished. The layers of the cerebellum are well pronounced. The vessels of the base of the brain are normal. The subcutaneous fat of the body is well-developed. The internal organs are properly arranged. The pericardial sac contained up to 20 cm3 of cloudy yellow liquid. The size of the heart is 12 x 10 x 5.5 cm. When sectioned, the cardiac muscle is dark red in color. The thickness of the left ventricle is 1.8 cm and the right is 0.5 cm. The right and left sections of the heart contained up to 200 cm3 of dark liquid blood. The valves of the heart, aorta and pulmonary artery are thin, smooth and shiny. The coronary vessels of the heart are free, smooth and passable. The internal surface of the aorta is smooth and clean. The surface of the lungs is pink-red in color and dough-like when palpated. When sectioned the lung tissue is dark red in color; when the section is pressed there is an abundant flow of dark liquid blood and bloody liquid foam released. The lumen of the larynx and bronchi are clear. The mucosa of the esophagus, trachea and bronchi are blue-red in color. When sectioned the thyroid is fleshy and dark red in color. The sublingual bone is whole. The stomach contained traces of slimy brown yellow mass. The mucosa of the stomach is blue-red in color with a good expression of the folds. Along the surface of the folds of the stomach there are many small blood effusions and Vishnevsky spots. The stomach mucosa is swollen. When sectioned the pancreas is finely lobed and dark red in color. The surface of the liver is smooth and bright. The liver is 26 x 16 x 14 x 9 cm in size. When sectioned the liver tissue is dark cherry red in color and fool of blood and the hepatic pattern is poorly distinguished. The gallbladder contained 30 cm3 of (crossed) brown colored liquid. The mucosa of the gallbladder is velvety and green in color. The spleen is 9 x 6 x 3 in size. When sectioned the tissue of the spleen is dark in color. The spleen is limp, and its capsule is shriveled, and pulp is released with heavy scraping. The lumen of the small intestine contained a mucous mass of brown-yellow color. In the lumen of the large intestine there is a fecal mass of dark brown color. The mucosa of the intestines is blue-red in color. The surface of the kidneys is smooth and shiny. When sectioned the tissue of the kidneys is dark cherry red in color. The layers of the kidney are poorly defined. The size of the right kidney is 10 x 6 x 3.5 cm; the left is 10 x 5 x 3. The cortica and medulla (illegible) of the adrenal gland are well defined. The bladder contained up to 500 cm3 of cloudy yellow liquid. The mucosa of the bladder is bluish.

For chemical and histological study, pieces of the internal organs of the body were removed.

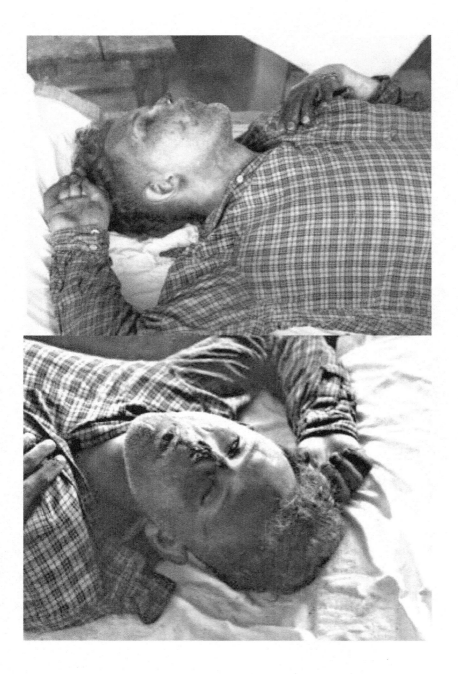

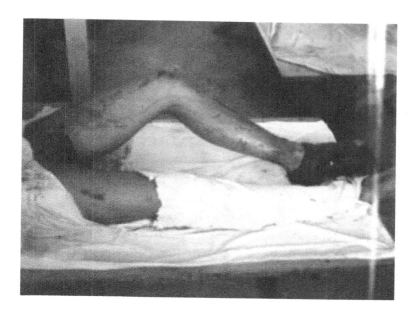

"Based on the data of investigation of the body of Krivonischenko Georgi Alekseevich, 23 years old, and considering the facts of the case, we think that the death of Krivonischenko was the result of the action of low temperature/freezing. This is evidenced by the swelling of the meninges, the blood-filled internal organs, the overfilling of the pericardium with dark liquid blood, the existence of Vishnevsky spots on the folds of the stomach, the overfilling of the bladder, the freezing of the fingers and toes and burns of the II-III degree by fire. Observed (written by hand, approximation). The lesions, grazes and skin wounds found during the external examination could have been the result of a fall or injury on rocks, ice, etc. The above-mentioned injuries were inflicted on Krivonischenko during life, the agonal state, and after death. The data of the investigation of the body of Krivonischenko provide the basis to suggest that he ate only 6-8 hours before the time of death. No presence of alcohol was found during the examination. The death was violent and accidental."

external examination

On the examination table is the body of a man of proper constitution.

The body is posed with the arms deviated at the shoulder joints, and the forearms are bent at the elbows in the horizontal position. The fingers are knuckled and placed on the chest. The head of the body is bent slightly to the back, the legs are bent at the pelvic and knee joints, and the toes are directed inside with the big toes touching each other. On the lower third portion of the left forearm there is a Zvezda-brand watch; the hands of the watch show 5 hours, 31 minutes.

The body is clothed in a fur jacket without sleeves covered in blue cotton material with dark grey fur, a blue woolen sweater, and a red cotton checked shirt with dark grey checks [and] three buttons, the top two of which are unbuttoned. The cuffs are buttoned by one button. The chest pocket contained a package of Streptocyde with four tablets. The body has a blue knitted sleeveless jacket. The body is wearing brown knitted ski trousers with fleece on an elastic support; underneath them are blue-green flannel sports pants with an elastic support and black satin briefs. On the right foot there is a white woolen sock; underneath it there are brown cotton socks. On the left leg there is a brown cotton knee sock.

The length of the body is 175 centimeters; it is of good nutrition with well-developed muscle groups. Postmortem lividity of bluish red color is evident on the posterior surface of the neck, trunk and extremities. Rigor mortis has resolved in the muscle groups of the joints. The hair on the head is light blond hair is up to 7 cm long, and with a box haircut. The forehead is high and reclining. In the

In the area of the forehead on the frontal eminence there is a scratch of brown red color and some stiffened density rising above the epidermal surface. The eyebrows are thick and light blond. The facial skin is of a bluish red color. The eyes are slightly opened; on the upper eyelids there are small scratches of brown-red color. The cornea is opaque, the iris is grey, and the pupils are widened. The nasal arch is straight. On the nasal arch and tip there is a section of brown-red color and parchment density sized 2 x 1.5 cm. In the area of both jowls there are scratches of brown-red color under dry crust sized 3 x 1.5 x 1 cm and 3 x 0.5 cm on the left and small scratches on the right. The lips are of bluish-purple color and covered in clotted blood. The mucosa of the gums is of pale grey color. On the upper jaw the teeth are white, pale, and thin; on the lower jaw the central incisor is absent without alteration of the gums' mucosa. The ear conches are of bluish pink color and oval shaped. In the area of the left cheek there are small dark brown scratches of parchment density. The orifices of the nose and mouth are clear. The neck is without particularities.

The chest is cylindrically shaped. The stomach is located below the chest level. The external genitals are properly formed. The rectum is clean. In the right and left area of the knee joints there are dark red scratches sized 1 x 0.5 cm and 0.5 by 0.5 cm of parchment density without hemorrhage into the surrounding tissue. There are scratches of brown-red color in the area of the left ankle joint on the anterior lateral and on the posterior surfaces of both ankles hollowed over the surface of the skin and also on the (illegible) skin, sized 1 x 0.5 cm and up to 3 x 2.5 cm with hemorrhaging into the underlying soft tissues. In the area of the scratches there is one laceration. In the lower third of the right leg there is graze wound 4 x 2 cm in size, and on the outer lateral surface in the lower third of the right forearm on the palm surface there are small dark red scratches of parchment density. The back of the right hand is of purple grey color. In the area of the wrist joints and between the phalangeal joints the soft tissue is of brown purple color of parchment density covered by dry crusts with hemorrhaging into the underlying tissues. The left hand is of brown purple color with dark red scratches, of parchment density, sized 1 x 0.5 cm, up to 2 x 0.2 cm. (illegible) of skin in the area of back surface of second and fourth fingers. In the area of the palm surface of the second and fifth fingers there is a skin wound of irregular linear shape with regular edges located transverse to the length of the fingers; the surface wounds are up to 0.1 (or 0.2 – note) cm deep. The skeletal bones and cartilages are intact upon palpation.

Internal examination

The skin of the scalp on the inner surface is wet, juicy, and of a shiny pale red color; the bones of the vault and the base of the scull are whole, the dura matter is bluish and filled with blood, the pia matter is opaque and engorged, cerebral gyri are (illegible), flattened, and the brain matter is a jelly-like mass of greenish-red color. The grey and white matter are poorly differentiated. The contours of the cerebral ventricles are not detected. The pattern of the cerebellum matter is poorly differentiated. The vessels of the brain base show no particularities. The subcutaneous fatty tissue of the body is well developed. The pleural cavities are free, and the pericardium contained up to ?0 cm3 of amber liquid. The heart is sized (illegible)2 x 10 x 7 cm and the surface is slightly covered in fat. When sectioned, the cardiac muscle is dark red. The thickness of the left ventricle muscle is 2 cm, and the thickness of the right ventricle muscle is 0.7 cm. The right and left halves of the heart contained up to 250 cm3 of liquid dark blood. The valves of the heart, aorta and pulmonary artery are smooth, thin, shiny, and of pale red color. The orifice of the coronary arteries is free; and the lumen of the arteries is expanded and well-passable. The internal surface of the aorta is smooth and clean, and the width of the aortic arch over the valves is 8 cm. The surface of the lungs isluish red and is dough-like during *palpation. The tissue of the lungs when sectioned is of dark red color; when pressing on the surface of the section there is the secretion of a great amount of liquid dark blood and foamy bloody liquid. The lumen of the throat and bronchi is free. The mucosa of the esophagus, trachea and bronchi is of bluish red color. The thyrohyals are intact. The thyroid gland in this section is dark red and meaty. The stomach contained about 100 cm3 of a liquid mucosal mass of brown-red color. The gastric mucosa is of purple-red color, engorged, and with well-expressed folds; on the upper surface of the gastric folds on the mucosare is large amount of small Vishnevsky spots hemorrhages. The smell from the gastric content is sour. The spleen is small lobular when sectioned and of purple-red color. In the lumen of the small intestine there is a mucosal mass of reddish color; the intestinal mucosa is of bluish red color. In the colon there are semi-formed feces of light brown color. The intestinal mucosa is pale purple. The spleen is feeble during palpation, its capsule is shrunk, and the size of the spleen is 13 x 7 x 2 cm. When sectioning the splenic tissue is of dark cherry color, the pulp gives (illegible) from the surface of the section there is large scrape. The liver at the surface is smooth and clean with a size of 26 x 16 x 11 x 10 cm, (illegible) when sectioned the hepatic tissue is of brown-cherry color and full blooded; the hepatic pattern is poorly defined. The gall bladder contained up to 30 cm3 of olive liquid, and the gall bladder mucosa is velvety and brown. The kidneys are smooth and shiny at the surface and the capsule is easily removed from the kidneys. The size of the right kidney is 10 x 5 x 3.5 cm, and the size of the left kidney is (illegible) x 5 x 3.5 cm. When sectioned the kidney tissue is of dark cherry color, the cortex and medulla layers are poorly differentiated, and the adrenals layers are well-differentiated. The bladder contained (illegible) liters of opaque light-yellow liquid. The mucosa of the bladder is of pale grey color. The examination of the body established no presence of alcohol.*

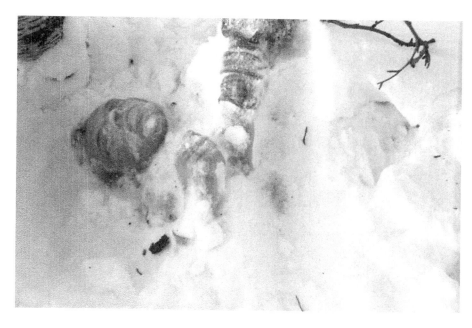

His Hands are not as bruised or cut as expected.

"Based on the data discovered (added by hand) from the examination of the body of Igor Alekseevich Dyatlov, 23 years old, and considering the circumstances of the case, we think Dyatlov died as the result of hypothermia/freezing signified by the oedema of the meninges, the sharp hyperaemia of the internal organs, the filling of the heart cavities with liquid dark blood, the presence of Vishnevsky spots on the gastric mucosa, the overfilled bladder, and III- and IV-grade cold injury of the extremities. The damage discovered (note: the word is handwritten) during the external examination in the form of graze wounds, scratches and skin wounds were caused by a blunt tool and may have happened as the result of a fall and bruising by stone, ice, etc. The above-mentioned damage was caused both during life, as well as in the agonal and post-mortem states. The above-mentioned injuries are light and not damaging to health. The data of the examination of the body of Dyatlov shows that his last meal was 6-8 hours before death. The investigation discovered no presence of alcohol. The cause of death is by violence/accident."

MEDICAL-FORENSIC EXAMINATION OF   KOLMOGOROVA
Zinaida Alekseevna, 22

external examination

On the examination table is a body of a woman: both of the upper limbs are bent at the elbows. The left lower limb is more straightened at the knee and hip. Both limbs are joined together and intersect one another in the area of the lower third of the right leg and the inside of the left knee. The toes are stretched and lowered downwards.

The body is dressed as follows: on the head is a red wool hat tied at the chin with a bow. Under the hat is a blue knitted hat attached to the hair with a clip. A blue wool sweater worn on the left with the left cuff torn. Under this is a cotton checked shirt with long sleeves and one closed left pocket; the left sleeve is closed at the cuff. The color of the checked shirt is black, green with red squares. Under the checked shirt on the left side of the chest is a military style defensive mask. Under the checked shirt is a light red woolen sweater worn on the left side with a light red to blue transverse stripe. On the left and right sleeves are two patches, one made from a brown sock and the other from blue cotton fabric. A knitted shirt with long blue arms. A black satin brassiere fastened with two buttons. Baize ski sport pants with a buckle on the hip and closed buttons. At the bottom, the cuffs of the pants are not buttoned; there are three tears on the right pant leg with a depth of 0.5 cm, 1.2 cm, and 0.3 cm. Blue cotton sports pants with (illegible) internal pockets, the buckles on the hips are unbuttoned. In the right pocket is a brown comb with two broken teeth. In the (illegible) pocket there is a black shoestring. At the bottom of the (illegible) on elastic. Knitted women's fleece leggings of an indeterminable color. Black ladies cotton tights with elastic. Swimming trunks with a four-button closure. On the legs are brown wool (illegible) with fur insoles; under them are blue and brown woolen socks.

The body is 162 cm long, of good nutrition and with well-developed muscle groups. There are blue and purple spots on the back surface of the body. Rigor mortis has resolved in the muscle groups of the joints. On the head is dark blond hair tied in two braids connected with two red silk ribbons. The length of the hair is up to 30 cm. The forehead is high and sloping towards the posterior. The skin of the face and hands is purple-red in color. In the area of the right frontal eminence there is a dark-red 2 x 1.5-cm abrasion that is solid when palpated. Next to this is a pale-colored spot with a size of 3 x 2 cm that reaches the right eyebrow. In the right temporomalor area is an irregularly formed? x 5 cm graze wound of dark red-brown color. The eyebrows are narrow and black. On the upper eyelid of the left and right eyes there is a piece of grazed skin of dark red color measuring 5 x 1 cm and 0.5 x 0.5 cm. The left eye is half open, the cornea is cloudy, and the iris is light brown in color. There are Lyarshe spots on the cornea of the left eye. The mucous membrane of the eyelids is red. The bridge of the nose is slightly arched. On the arch of the nose there is a 1 x 0.7-cm abrasion. On the tip of the nose there is the same parchment abrasion with an area of 2 x 1 cm. In the area of the zygomatic arch, cheeks and chin there are a number of abrasions of different forms and magnitudes under dry brown crust with sizes from 6 x 2 cm to? x 1 cm and smaller. The lips are blue-red in color and hydropic. The mouth is slightly opened. The teeth are white and even. The tongue is completely in the mouth behind the teeth; the mucous membrane of the gums is blue-pink in color. The openings of the mouth, nose and ears are clean. The ears are oval in shape and pink in color. The neck is normal. The chest is cylindrical in form. The breasts are medium in size and dough-like. The nipples protrude above the surface of the breasts. The nipples and areola are light grey in color. The stomach is located at the level of the chest. The external genitals are properly formed; their mucous membrane is of blue-pink color. The hymen is ring shaped with free edges. The natural orifice of the hymen allows for an adult pinky finger to pass. There is no vaginal discharge. On the back of the right and left hands in the area of the wrist and interphalangeal joints are brown-red abrasions that are solid when palpated measuring 1.5 x 1 to 0.3 x 4 cm. There is an irregularly shaped 3 x 2.2-cm wound on the base of the third finger on the right hand with an angle facing the terminal phalanx with uneven borders and a scalped skin graft. The terminal phalanx of fingers 1-5 on the left hand are solid when palpated, dry, and of a brown-purple color. There is a well-shown venous network on the surface of both upper limbs. The lower limbs have no visible damage and are pinkish red in color. On the surface of the area of the lower back on the right side of the abdomen there is a graze wound of bright red color in the form of a strip sized 26 x 6 cm. The rest of the body and limbs are of a pale red color. There is a very pronounced venous system on the legs and feet.

Internal examination

The skin flaps of the scalp are moist, rich and brilliantly red in color. The bones of the fornix and the base of the skull are whole. The dura matter is blue-grey in color and full-blooded. The pia is muddy and swollen. The gyrus and sulcus of the brain are smooth and flat. The contours of the lateral vesicles of the brain are indistinguishable. The grey brain matter is poorly differentiated from the white. The brain matter appears as a jelly-like mass with a blue-red color. The cerebral pattern is poorly differentiated. The blood vessels of the base of the brain are normal. The body's subcutaneous fat is sufficiently developed. The internal organs are in the correct position; the lungs freely lie in the pleural cavity. The pericardium contained around 30 cm3 of dark liquid blood; the heart is 12 x 10.6 cm in size and its surface is covered in fat. The valves of the heart, aorta and pulmonary arteries are smooth, thin and brilliant. The coronary vessels are free and passable. The internal surface of the aorta is smooth and clean. The width of the arch of the aorta above the valve is 8 cm.

The surface of the lungs is blue-red in color and dough-like when palpated. When sectioned the lung tissue is dark red in color; when pressed an abundance of bloody liquid and dark liquid blood is emitted. The lumen of the larynx and bronchi are free. The mucous membrane of the trachea and bronchi are blue-red in color. The sublingual bone is intact. When sectioned the thyroid gland is blue-red in color. The gastric cavity contained traces of a dirty-yellow-colored frosty mucus mass. The mucous membrane of the stomach is grey-red in color with the folds well-exhibited. On the upper surface of the gastric mucosare are Vishnevsky spot hemorrhages. When sectioned, the pancreas is pinkish red in color and finely lobular. The surface of the liver is smooth and bright; the size of the liver is 24 x 15 x 11 x 8 cm. When sectioned the liver tissue is brown-cherry in color with a poor differentiation of the hepatic pattern, and dramatically full of blood. The gallbladder contained up to 30 cm3 of olive-colored liquid. The mucous membrane of the gallbladder is velvety and brown in color. The spleen is limp when palpated and its capsule is shriveled. When sectioned, the tissue of the spleen is dark cherry in color. The slurry from the surface of the section is given with much scraping. The size of the spleen is 9 x 6.2 x 2 cm. The lumen of the small intestine contained a mucous mass that was dirty yellow in color. The mucous membrane of the intestine is blue-red in color. In the lumen of the large intestine there is a fecal mass of dark brown color. The surface of the kidneys is smooth and bright; the kidney capsule is easily removed. When sectioned the kidney tissue is dark cherry colored. The cortical renal medulla is poorly differentiated. The layers of the adrenal gland are well differentiated. The size of the right kidney is 8 x 5 x 3 cm; the left is 8 x 5 x 2.5 cm. The uterus is small and solid when palpated. When sectioned the tissue is light grey in color. In the opening of the uterus there are traces of pale-red slime. When sectioned the appendages are normal. The bladder contained up to 300 cm3 of cloudy yellow liquid. The mucous membrane of the bladder was light pink in color.

Parts of the internal organs were removed for chemical and histological analysis. The presence of alcohol was not found upon examination of the body.

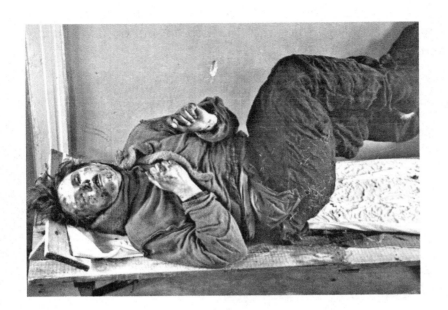

"Based on the investigation of the body of Kolmogorova Zinaida Alekseevna, 22 years old, and taking into account the circumstances of the case, we feel that the death of Kolmogorova was the result of cool temperatures/freezing, as evidenced by the swelling of the meninges, the dramatic plethora of the internal organs, the dark liquid blood in the heart cavities, the Vishnevsky spots on the gastric mucosa, and the fourth-degree frostbite on the third terminal phalanges of the fingers; the injuries found on Kolmogorova's body in the form of abrasions and skin wounds were caused by a blunt instrument and the result of a fall and injuries on rocks, ice and snow. The above-mentioned injuries occurred while Kolmogorova was alive, in the agonal state, and posthumously. The investigation of the body of Komogorova allows for the basis of theory that she last ate 6-8 hours before the time of death. Alcohol was not detected during the investigation. Kolmogorova's virginity is still intact. The cause of death was violent and accidental."

External examination

On the examination table is a male body of proper constitution clothed as follows: a black zippered fustian ski jacket with right and left breast pockets with the unbuttoned cuffs still intact. There are defects in the fabric of the upper left arm of the jacket measuring 25 x 12 x 13 cm; the edges of the fabric in this area are burned. There is a tear measuring 7-8 cm on the right elbow of the jacket. Above the jacket is a brown fleece knitted sweater, and under this is a second ragged sweater of grey color and a checked shirt with blue, red and black squares and two breast pockets. On the right pocket is an English letter, and inside it is a key to a lock; the collar and the cuffs of the checked shirt are closed. In the left pocket is a piece of brown paper and wrapping from a packet of 'Codeine with Soda.'

A pale grey worn-out fleece undershirt. Canvas one-piece khaki pants with elastic support. In the right pants pocket is a soaked pack of matches. At the bottom of the pants there are cracked metal straps. Underneath them are baize ski pants with lateral buckles and a handkerchief in the pocket. On the feet are dirty white home-knitted wool socks, parts of which are burned, and brown cotton socks. On the left leg there are three brown cotton socks with a gauze bandage underneath them at the ankle joint. Pale grey underpants matching the shirt, and blue satin underwear.

The body is 174 cm in length, of proper constitution, and good nutrition.

Cadaverous crimson spots are located all over on the surface of the back-right side of the trunk and the appendages. Rigor mortis has resolved in the muscle groups of the joints. The skin covering the face of the body is yellow grey with hints of purple. On the head is dark blond hair with a length of up to 10 cm. In the superior postcranial areare is a part where hair is missing (cadaverous hair slide) The forehead is low and straight. There are no eyebrows. The skin is missing in the area of the eye sockets and eyebrows, exposing the facial bone; the soft tissue around the edge of the exposed bone is limp, smooth and slightly raised. The eyeballs are wrinkled and sunken into the eye sockets. The bridge of the nose is straight; the nose cartilage is soft when palpated and has unusual mobility. The base of the nose is flattened with the nostrils compressed.

There is a defect in the soft tissue in the area of the right cheek measuring 4 x 5.5 cm of uneven oval form with pressed smooth drawn-out margins. The bones of the lower jaw appear at the bottom of the defect of the soft tissue. The mouth is wide open, and the teeth are even and white. The tongue is completely in the mouth. The soft tissue of the face is thin, flaccid and of a dirty grey color. There is a wound of undetermined shape measuring 3 x 1.5 x 0.5 cm behind the right ear in the area of the mastoid process that penetrates into the mastoid process. Around the defect located on the right cheek in the area of the lower jaw, the soft tissue is of a purple-green color.

The neck is long and thin, and deformed in the area of the thyroid cartilage. The thorax is rectangular in shape. The surface layer of the epidermis is slipping from the skin covering the chest.

There is 'bath skin' of a pale grey color in the area of the fingers. The fingers are partially bent.

The stomach is located at the level of the chest. The right thigh is adducted to the left. In the area of the external surface of the right thigh there is an area of pitted soft tissue measuring 25 x 15 cm without hemorrhaging to the surrounding soft tissue.

The external genitals are properly formed and without any abnormalities. The opening of the anus is clear.

There is pale grey 'bath skin' in the area of the foot. The bones of the limbs are whole when palpated. On the inner surface of the left knee there is diffuse bleeding into the underlying tissue.

Internal examination

The skin flaps of the scalp are moist and of pale red color. The bones of the fornix of the brain and the base of the skull are whole. The dura matter has a bluish coloration and is sufficiently filled with blood. The pia matter is thin and cloudy. The gyrus and sulcus are poorly distinguished. The grey brain matter is poorly differentiated from the white. The ventricle contours of the brain are indistinguishable. The brain matter is of a gelatinous consistency. The blood vessels at the base of the brain are normal. The subcutaneous fat of body is sufficiently developed. The internal organs are properly arranged. The pleural cavity contained up to 500 cm3 of bloody fluid. The pericardium contained up to 13 cm3 of amber fluid.

The surface of the heart is lightly covered in fat. The size of the heart is 13 x 12 x 5 cm. The cardiac muscle is dark red in color when sectioned. The right and left halves of the heart contained up to 100 cm3 of dark liquid blood. The valves of the heart, the aorta and the pulmonary artery are slightly thickened along the coaptation line. The coronary vessels of the heart are freely passable. The internal surface of the aorta is smooth and clear. The width of the aortic arch above the valve is 7 cm. The surface of the lungs is blue-red in color and soft when palpated. When sectioned, the tissue is dark red in color. When the surface of the section is pressed, a large amount of foamy bloody liquid is released.

The openings of the larynx and bronchi are free. The hyoid bone is intact. The neck muscles and intervertebral cervical spine appear as remnants of soft tissue and are green-grey in color (putrefactive changes)

The stomach contained up to 100 cm3 of a pale red slimy mass. The gastric mucosa was swollen, loose, with well-defined folding and was blue red in color. When sectioned the pancreas was lobular and yellow-blue in color. The surface of the liver was faint and smooth. The size of the liver was 23 x 15 x 12 x 7 cm. When sectioned the liver tissue was brown with a poorly discernible liver pattern. The gall bladder contained up to 5 cm3 of dark brown liquid; its mucous membrane was of a brown-green color. The lumen of the small intestine contained a pale red mucosal mass with hints of yellow. The lumen of the large intestine contained fecal matter that was brownish green in color. The mucous membrane of the intestine was blue-red in color and loose when palpated. When sectioned the tissue was dark cherry red in color. The surface of the kidneys was smooth and shiny; the capsule was easily removed from the kidneys. When sectioned, the tissue of the kidneys was dark red in color. The cortex and medulla were well-distinguished. The layers of the adrenal gland were poorly distinguished. The bladder contained up to 700 cm3 of murky yellow liquid. The mucous membrane of the bladder was blue.

For chemical and histological study, pieces of the internal organs of the body were removed.

"Based on the examination of the body of Kolevatov, I think that his death was the result of low temperature. The injuries that appear on Kolevatov's body in the area of his head – defects in the soft tissue and the 'bath skin' – are the result of post-death changes in the body, which was in water for some time before it was found. The cause of death of Kolevatov was through violence."

Medical-Forensic Examination of Aleksander Alekseevich Zolotaryov, 37

External examination:

On the examination table there is a male body, clothed as follows: on the head there is a black fur winter cap with ear flaps decorated with black fur and a red woollen ski cap with three light stripes. A checked worn woollen scarf of brown and blue color with an opened breast pin. A tourist mask of baize and green denim with an elastic support. A very worn fur waistcoat made of black sheep skin. A buttoned brown baize sports jacket. The left chest pocket lacks a button. Out of the three buttons in the neck area, the two top ones are unbuttoned. The left sleeve is buttoned by one button, and the right is buttoned. A slightly worn black cotton sweater. A cotton sports t-shirt with blue sleeves and a woven cotton cherry-blossom t-shirt. Khaki denim romper trousers with two pockets attached. The right pocket contains an onion bulb and coins of three, five, and 15 kopecks. Black quilted felt boots with leather soles with woolen brown socks in them. There is one sock on the right foot and two stitched socks on the left foot; one is woolen and the other is cotton. In the inner chest pocket of the romper there are a brush and a ball of yarn. There is a rolled-up newspaper in the posterior pocket of the rompers. Under the rompers there are torn baize blue ski trousers with the three buttons on the waist not buttoned; the buttons on the cuffs are buttoned. The internal pockets of the trousers are empty. Underneath them are similar trousers but with an elastic support. The pockets of the trousers include pieces of newspaper and five coins: two of 15 kopecks, and two of 2 kopecks and 10 kopecks. Gray cotton trunks are worn inside-out over blue satin briefs. There is a compass in the left hand of the body.

Findings after the removal of the clothes: the body is male of satisfactory nutrition and proper constitution with a length of 172 cm. Postmortem lividity of purple-grey color are plentiful on the posterior surface of the neck, trunk and extremities and on the lateral surface of the chest on the right side. Rigor mortis is resolved in the muscle groups of the joints. In the frontal temporal area is a section of alopecia.

The hair present slides from the scalp when touched. The remnants of the hair are black and up to 10 cm long. In the right temporal areare is a soft tissue defect of irregular shape sized 8 x 6 cm with thinned, slightly rumpled edges baring the temporal bone. The facial skin is of grayish green color. The forehead is low and retreating. The eyebrows are absent. In the area of the brows and eye sockets there is a round-shaped soft tissue defect sized 7 x 6 cm with thinned edges and bared facial skull bones. The eye sockets are glaring. The eyeballs are absent. The nasal dorsum is straight. The nasal bones and cartilages are whole when palpated. The nose is flattened at the base. The nasal orifices are constricted. The upper lip has the remnants of a light brown mustache and the lips are pale grey. On the right side of the upper jaw there are two dental crowns and a tooth of white metal; on the lower jaw there are four dental crowns of white metal. The mouth is opened wide. The oral mucosa is of greenish grey color (rot-induced changes). The orifices of the mouth and ear passages are clean. The neck is long and thin. The chest is cylindrically shaped. The stomach is located below the chest level. The external genitals are properly formed. There are signs of defecation from the rectum. 'Bath skin' is present in the area of the hands and toes. The skin of the trunk and extremities is grayish blue with the sliding of the epidermis. The fingers are semi-bent. On the reverse of the right hand near the base of the thumb there is the tattoo 'Gena' ('Гена'). On the reverse of the right forearm in the medium third there is a tattoo of a beetroot [picture] and 'letters + C'; the reverse side of the left forehand has a tattoo with the image 'G.S.' DAERMMUAZUAYA' ('Г.С.' ДАЕРММУАЗУАЯ'), a five-point star and the letter 'C', the letters Г+С+П = Д' and the number 1921.'

<u>*Internal examination:*</u>

The skin of the scalp from the internal surface is wet, dim, and pale red. The bones of the cranial vault and base are intact. The dura matter is bluish green and of poor blood saturation. The pia matter is thin and opaque. The brain gyri are poorly defined. The grey and white matter are poorly differentiated. The contours of the brain ventricles are not defined. The vessels of the cranial base show no particularities. The subcutaneous fatty tissue is satisfactorily developed. The position of the internal organs is proper. The pleural cavities contained up to one litre of liquid dark blood. The pericardium contained up to 15 cm3 of opaque amber liquid. The heart is sized 13 x 10 x 6 cm. The cardiac muscle is dark red when sectioned. The right and left halves of the heart contained up to 50 cm3 of liquid dark blood. The aortic heart valve and pulmonary artery valve are slightly thickened on the adjacent line. The coronary vessels of the heart are free and passable. The internal surface of the aorta is smooth and clean. The lungs are bluish red on the surface and fluffy upon palpation. The pulmonary tissue is of dark cherry color when sectioned. When pressed, a large amount of foamy bloody liquid is secreted from the surface of the section. The lumen of the throat and bronchi is free. The sublingual bone is intact. The mucosa of the esophagus, trachea and bronchi is bluish red. The stomach contained traces of pale red mucosal mass. The gastric mucosa is bluish red with poorly defined folds. When sectioned, the pancreas is finely lobular with a red yellowish color. The liver is dim and smooth at the surface. When sectioned the tissue is brown-red with bluish shade and poorly distinguished hepatic patterns. The liver 26 x 15 x 10 x 7 cm in size. The gall bladder contained traces of brown liquid. Its mucosa is brown. The spleen is feeble during palpation. Its capsule is shrunk. The size of the spleen is 10 x 7 x 3 cm. The spleen tissue is of dark cherry color when sectioned. The pulp from the sectioned surface is scratched well. In the lumen of the small intestine there is a mucosal mass of dirty yellow color. The intestinal mucosa is of a bluish green color. The lumen of the colon contains fecal masses of brown-yellow color. The intestinal mucosa is bluish grey. The kidneys on the surface are smooth and dim; the capsule of the kidneys is easily removed. The size of the right kidney is 10 x 6 x 3 cm; the size of the left kidney is 9.5 x 6 x 3 cm. The cortex and medullar layer of the kidney are poorly differentiated. When sectioned, the kidney tissue is dark red in color. The cortex and medullar layers of the adrenals are poorly differentiated. The bladder contained up to 500 cm3 of opaque yellowish liquid. After the removal of the organ complex from the thoracic and abdominal cavity, the fracture of the II, III, IV, V, and VI ribs was detected on the right on the adsternal and mid-axillary line with hemorrhaging into the adjacent intercostal muscles.

Parts of the internal organs of the body were taken for chemical and histological examination.

"Based on the examination of the body of Zolotaryov, 37 years old, I think that he died due to multiple fractures of the right ribs with internal hemorrhaging to the pleural cavity while at a low temperature. The above-mentioned multiple fractures of Zolotaryov's ribs with hemorrhaging into the pleural cavity were caused in vivo as an effect of a high-power impact to the chest of Zolotaryov at the moment of his fall, squeezing or throwing. The damage of the soft tissue in the area of Mr. Zolotaryov's head and the presence of bath skin in the area of fingers and upper and lower extremities are postmortem changes in the body of Zolotaryov, which was underwater before it was found. Zolotaryov died as a result of violence."

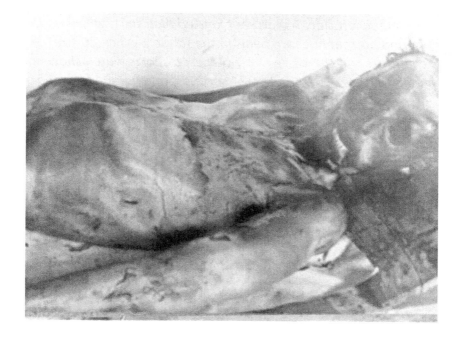

Medical-Forensic Examination of Thibeaux-Brignolle Nikolay Vasilyevich, 23

External examination

On the examination table is a male body clothed as follows: the head is covered by a tightly tied green woolen sports cap with three round holes sized 3 x 3 cm located in the front. A khaki canvas fur helmet with a zipper fastener [like a flying helmet]; the helmet is drawn by a cord. A green canvas sheepskin jacket with a zipper and two pockets. In the right pocket there are grey gloves. In the left pocket are 10, 20, and 2 kopeck coins; two folded pieces of paper; and a comb. A ragged wool sweater is worn on the left side. A worn-out knitted blue shirt, which on the right and bottom has torn ovals in the fabric 2 x 3 cm in size. On the left forearm there are two watches: a sports watch showing the time 8 hours, 14 minutes, 24 seconds, and a Pobeda brand watch showing the time 8 hours, 39 minutes. The legs are covered with practically new grey felt boots (valenki). On the right leg are white hand knitted wool socks; the same socks are also on the left leg. There are crumpled brown wool socks located in the soles of the corresponding felt boots. The body is wearing warm woolen winter pants, the cuffs of which are fasted by a leather belt with a metal buckle. Under these pants are blue cotton sports pants and black satin underwear. In the pocket (crossed) of the outer pants a white metal button and a metal chain from a wall clock were found.

After the removal of the clothes, the following was found: a male body of proper constitution and good nutrition, 174 cm long. The body has purple green spots on the posterolateral surface of the chest, neck and extremities. Rigor mortis has resolved in the muscle groups of the joints. The skin of the face, body and limbs is of a red-green color seeping from the surface layer of the epidermis. There is hair on the head with a length of 8 cm. The forehead is high and sloping backwards and there are thick black eyebrows. The eyes are closed; the eyeballs are sunk far into their sockets. The cornea is cloudy and dry, the iris is light green, and the mucosal membrane of the eyelid is of a pale grey color. The bridge of the nose is straight. (crossed) The bones of the nose are intact when touched. On the upper left jaw there is a defect in the soft tissue, which has an irregular oval shape with a size of 3 x 4 cm with drawn out, convoluted borders exposing the alveolar edge of the upper jaw, the teeth are white and even. The mouth is open. The lips have a pale grey color. The tongue is in the mouth. The mucous membrane of the tongue and mouth are of a dirty green color. On the cheeks, chin and upper lip there is black hair with a length of up to 1 cm. The openings of the mouth, nose and ear are clean. The neck is long and thin. The chest is cylindrical. The stomach is located below the chest. The dorsum of the hands and fingers are of a pale brown color and of parchment density; the fingers are bent at the joints. In the area of the fingers there is 'bath skin' of a pale grey color with the rejection of the nail plate. There is a 10 x 12 cm blue-green diffuse ecchymoma in the area of the right shoulder on the antero-internal surface at the lower middle and bottom thirds. In the area of the ecchymomare is hemorrhaging into the surrounding soft tissue. The external genitalia are normal. The opening of the anus is clear. In the area of the toes there is 'bath skin' of a pale grey color.

Internal examination

Skin pieces of the scalp from the internal surface are juicy and dull. There is an indication of hemorrhaging from the right temple into the right temporal muscle with diffuse saturation. After dissection of the right temporal muscle determined that there was a depressed fracture in the right temporal bregmatic area on an area measuring 9 x 7 cm with a bone defect on the temporal lobe measuring 3 x 3.5 x 2 cm. This section of the bone is sunken into the cranial cavity and is located on the dura matter. After the extraction of the brain matter, in the middle cranial pit a multi-splintered fracture of the right temporal lobe was discovered with the diffusion of the cracked bone to the anterior cranial fossa and the supraorbital region of the frontal bone. A second crack runs along the front surface of the sella turcica in the area of the pterygoid processes, venturing into the interior of the underlying bone, then proceeding to the middle cranial fossa on the left with the separation of the bone from 0.1 to 0.4 cm. The dura mater, corresponding to the site of the fracture, is sharply full-blooded with the fullness of the brain substance of the right cerebral hemisphere, which differs by a more greenish-colored color. The fissures and convolutions of the brain are poorly differentiated. The brain's grey matter is poorly differentiated from the white. The contours of the ventricles of the brain are indistinguishable. The brain is a jelly-like mass with a dirty red color. On the whole, the length of the crack in the area of the base of the skull is 17 cm. In addition, there is asymmetry due to the compression fracture of this area. The subcutaneous tissue of the torso is sufficiently developed. The internal organs are positioned correctly. The pleural cavity is free. The pericardium contained up to 10 cm3 of red turbid liquid. The heart is 13 x 12 x 5.5 cm in size with the surface slightly covered in fat. The cardiac muscle is dark red when sectioned and soft when palpated. The thickness of the left ventricle is 1.8 cm, and the right is 0.6 cm. The right and left parts of the heart contain dark liquid blood in the form of 'dry heart.' The valves of heart, the aorta and the pulmonary artery are smooth, shiny, and slightly thickened. The coronary vessels of the heart are free and passable. The internal surface of the aorta is smooth and clean. The width of the aortic arch above the valves is 8.5 cm. The lungs are blue-red (blue is typed on top of another text - ed.) on the surface, creamy on touch. When sectioned the lung tissue is of a dark red color. While palpated an abundance of foamy liquid is released. The larynx and bronchus clearance is free. The hyoid bone is intact. The mucosa of the esophagus, trachea and bronchi are blue-red in color. The ventricle contained up to 100 cm3 of mucous mass of a red-yellow color. The gastric mucosa has a blue-red color with good definition of the folds. When sectioned the pancreas is lobulated with a blue-red color. The surface of the liver is smooth, bright, and when sectioned its tissue has a brown-green color with hints of yellow. The hepatic pattern is poorly defined. The gall bladder contained traces of brown liquid; its mucosa was velvety brown. The size of the liver is 24 x 16 x 14 x 8 cm. The spleen is flaccid when palpated, its capsule is shriveled, and is sized 9 x 5 x 3 cm. When sectioned, the tissue of the spleen had a dark red color and gave a thick pulp when scraped. The lumen of the small intestine contained a slimy green mass with hints of brown. Partially formed fecal matter was found in the lumen of the large intestine. The intestinal mucosa had a blue-red color. The kidneys were smooth and shiny, and the capsule from the kidney is easily removed. When sectioned the kidneys were dark red; the cortex and the medulla of the kidneys were distinguishable. The size of the right kidney is 9 x 6 x 6 cm; the size of the left is 10 x 6 x 3 cm. The cortex and the medulla of the adrenal gland were poorly distinguished. The bladder was empty, and its mucous membrane was of blue color.

For chemical and histological examination, samples of the internal organs and right temporo-parietal bone were taken

.

On the basis of the examination of the body of Thibeaux-Brignolle, it is my opinion that his death was the result of a closed comminuted pressure fracture in the area of the base and the vault of the cranium with a prolific amount of bleeding under the meninges and brain matter while under low temperature. The above-mentioned extensive comminuted fracture of the base and the vault of the cranium are of in vivo origin and are the result of a great force with the subsequent falling, hurling and concussion of Thibeaux-Brignolle.

The corporal damage of the soft tissue in the area of the head and the 'bath skin' of the extremities are the result of post-mortem changes in the body of Thibeaux-Brignolle, which was found submerged in water after some time. The death of Thibeaux-Brignolle was a result of violence.

External examination:
On the section table there is a body of woman dressed as follows: head covered by a knitted helmet. A worn greyish-brown wool sweater with beige wool sweater underneath, checked shirt with buttoned sleeves. Yellow t-shirt with short sleeves, white cotton bra buttoned with three buttons. The body is wearing torn dark cotton trousers with an elastic waistband. The trousers are very torn and burned in places. Left leg – part of the leg and foot are covered with burned grey wool cloth from a jacket with its sleeve. On the left leg there is a torn grey woollen sock. On both legs there are torn blue cotton socks with grey wool machine knitted socks under them. Black cotton tights, torn in the crotch area, with an elastic waistband.

On the legs of the body there are light brown cotton stockings. The stocking from the left leg is removed, the right stocking is held with an elastic band. Grey ladies' belt with elastic supports. Satin briefs. The belt is buttoned with black buttons.

After the removal of the clothes there was found: a female body of proper constitution and good nutrition, 167 cm long. The post mortem lividity is of bluish grey color, particularly on the posterior and lateral surface of neck, body and extremities. Dark blond hair on the head, braided into one braid up to 50 cm long with a blue silk ribbon. The forehead is straight, retreating to the back.

The skin of the face is of yellowish-brown color. The soft tissue in the area of the supraorbital ridges, on the bridge of the nose, the eye sockets and left temporal-zygomatic area are all absent, exposing the facial skull bones. The eye sockets are glaring, the eyeballs are absent. The bones of the nasal bridge are intact, the nasal cartilage is flattened. There is an absence of the soft tissue from the upper lip on the right with thinning of its edges, exposing the alveolar edge of the upper jaw and teeth. The teeth are regular, intact. The tongue in the oral cavity is absent. The oral mucosa are of grayish green color.

The ear pinnae are oval. The orifices of mouth, nose and ear passages are clean. The neck is long and thin. The soft tissue in the neck area is flaccid when palpated. When palpating the neck, there is extraordinary mobility of the thyrohyal and thyroid cartilages. The chest is of cylindrical shape. The breasts are of medium size, full. The nipples and areoles are of pale brown color. The stomach is located at normal chest level. The external genitals are formed properly. The hymen is of ring-like shape with high rim, meaty. The natural orifice of the hymen allows the passage of adult's pinkie tip. The mucosa of the vagina is of purple-red color. On the external and anterior surface of the left thigh in the middle third there is diffuse bruising of bluish-purple color of 10 x 5 cm with deep skin hemorrhage. On the back of the hand there is soft tissue that is dense upon palpation, the fingers of the hands are semi-bent. The end phalanges of the fingers are covered with wrinkled 'bath skin' which is removed together with the nail plate. In the area of the feet and fingers the 'bath skin' is of pale grey color with purple shade. During palpation of the chest there is noted an extraordinary mobility of the ribs. In the area of the left temporal bone there is a soft tissue defect sized 4 x 4 cm with the bottom of the defect exposing the temporal bone.

Internal examination

The skin pieces of the scalp from the internal surface are wet, juicy and shiny. The bones of the skull vault and base are intact. The brain membrane is bluish from poor blood filling. The cerebral gyri convolutions are poorly defined. The grey brain matter is poorly differentiated from the white. The contours of the lateral brain ventricles are poorly defined. The vessels of the brain base are without particularity. The subcutaneous fatty tissue of the trunk is well developed. The position of the internal organs is regular, the pleural cavities contain up to one and a half litres of liquid dark blood. The pericardium contained up to 20 cubic cm of yellowish transparent liquid. The heart is sized 12 x 4 x 5 cm. In the area of the left ventricle there is an irregularly oval-shaped hemorrhage sized 4 x 4 cm with diffuse suffusion of the right ventricle muscle. The thickness of the left ventricle muscle is 1.4 cm, the right - 0.5 cm. In the right and left halves of the heart there was up to 50 cm3 of liquid dark blood. The cardiac valves of the aorta and pulmonary artery are smooth, thin, and shiny. The coronary vessels of the heart are freely passable. The internal surface of the aorta is smooth and clean. The lungs from the surface are of bluish-red color, fluffy during palpation. A section of lung tissue is of dark red color, during pushing from the surface there is plentiful foamy bloody liquid, the lumen of the bronchi is free. The thyrohyal is of extraordinary mobility (crossed), soft tissue adjacent to the sublingual bone is of dirty grey color. The diaphragm of the mouth and tongue is absent. The upper edge of the sublingual bone is bared. Esophagus mucosa and bronchial tracheas are of bluish-red color. The stomach contains up to 100 cm3 of dark brown mucosal mass. The gastric mucosa is porous, of bluish-red color. The pancreas is small and lobular when sectioned and is bluish-red. The liver from the surface is smooth and opaque. The size of the liver is 23 x 12 x 10 x 6 cm. When sectioned the tissue of the liver is of brownish red color with a poorly defined pattern. The gall bladder contains up to 5 cm3 of brown liquid. The mucosa of the gall bladder is velvety, brown. The spleen is flabby when palpated, and the channels are still wrinkled. The spleen size is 7 x 5 x 2 cm. In the lumen of the small intestine there is mucosal mass of dirty yellow color. In the lumen of the colon there are fecal masses of dirty green color. The intestinal mucosa is of bluish red color. The surface of the kidneys is smooth and shiny. The capsule is removed easily from the kidneys. The tissue of the kidneys when sectioned is of dark red color. The size of the right kidney is x 5 x 2 cm, the size of the left kidney is 9 x 5.5 x 2.3 cm. The cortex and medulla areas of the kidneys are well defined. The cortex and medulla area of the adrenals is poorly defined. The uterus upon section is pale grey, its lumen contains traces of pale-yellow mucosa. The ovaries and appendages are without particularities.

After the removal of the organ complex from the thoracic and abdominal cavity, the multiple bilateral fracture of the ribs was found on the right II, III, IV, V on the mid-clavicular and mid-axillary line; on the left there is a fracture of II, III, IV, V, VI, VII ribs on the mid-clavicular line. In the place of the rib fractures there are diffuse hemorrhages into the intercostal muscles.

In the area of the manubrium of the sternum on the right there is diffuse haemorrhaging.

Parts of the internal organs were taken from the body for chemical and histological study.

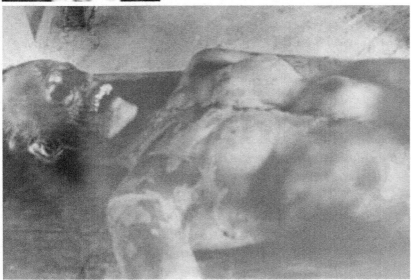

"Based on the forensic examination of the body of L. A. Dubinina I think that the death of Dubinina was caused by massive hemorrhage into the right ventricle, multiple bilateral rib fractures, and internal bleeding into the thoracic cavity.

The said damage was probably caused by an impact of great force causing severe closed lethal trauma to the chest of Dubinina. The trauma was caused during life and is the result of high force impact with subsequent fall, throw or bruise to the chest of Dubinina. Damage to the soft tissue of the head and 'bath skin' wrinkling to the extremities are the post-mortem changes (rot and decay) of Dubinina's body, which was underwater before it was found. The death of Dubinina is through violence."

END

catt dahman, a native Texan, is a prolific horror writer with Severed Press and J Ellington Ashton. She writes horror, has a crime series, and pens historical horror. A graduate of Texas A&M, she delves into the personalities of her characters and the depravity of the human mind. She has fifty novels available, and her works appear in several anthologies. With over thirty years of writing, one of her biggest accomplishments, is working in the area of extreme horror, an area that she was once told was out-of-reach because of her gender. She regularly participates in book-signings and conventions where she speaks at panel discussions and enjoys meeting horror fanatics.

cattd.com

jellingtonashton.com

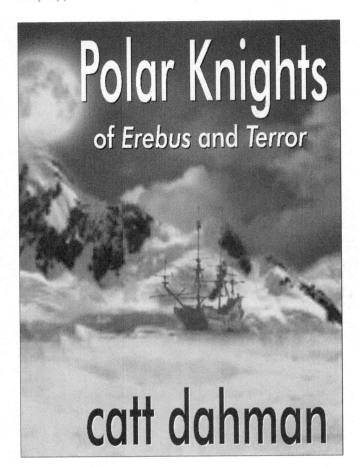

Polar Knights

of *Erebus* and *Terror*

catt dahman

Made in the USA
Coppell, TX
29 November 2019

12098723R00174